LIGUORI CATHOLIC BIBLE STUDY

Introduction
to the Bible

OVERVIEW, HISTORICAL CONTEXT, AND CULTURAL PERSPECTIVES

WILLIAM A. ANDERSON, DMIN, PHD

Liguori
LIGUORI, MISSOURI

Imprimi Potest:
Harry Grile, CSsR, Provincial
Denver Province, The Redemptorists

Imprimatur:
Printed with Ecclesiastical Permission and Approved for Private or Instructional Use

Nihil Obstat: Reverend Monsignor Kevin Quirk, JCD, JV
Censor Liborum
Imprimatur: + Michael J. Bransfield
Bishop of Wheeling-Charleston [West Virginia]
December 16, 2011

Published by Liguori Publications, Liguori, Missouri 63057
To order, call 800-325-9521, or visit liguori.org.

Library of Congress Cataloging-in-Publication Data
Anderson, William Angor, 1937-
   Introduction to the Bible : overview, historical context, and cultural perspectives / William A. Anderson.—1st ed.
   p. cm.
   ISBN 978-0-7648-2119-6
   1. Bible—Introductions. I. Title.
   BS475.3.A54 2012
   220.6'1—dc23

                                                                    2012001462

Liguori Publications, a nonprofit corporation, is an apostolate of the Redemptorists. To learn more about the Redemptorists, visit Redemptorists.com.

Printed in the United States of America
16 15 14 13 12 / 5 4 3 2
First Edition

Contents

About the Author

William A. Anderson, DMin, PhD, is a presbyter of the diocese of Wheeling-Charleston, West Virginia. A director of retreats and parish missions, professor, catechist, spiritual director, and a former pastor, he has written extensively on pastoral, spiritual, and religious subjects. Father Anderson earned his doctor of ministry degree from St. Mary's Seminary & University in Baltimore, and his doctorate in sacred theology from Duquesne University in Pittsburgh.

WORDS OF PRAISE

"This very useful catechetical work, *Introduction to the Bible*, provides an excellent and very accessible introduction to the study of Sacred Scripture. With the explanation and introduction to *lectio divina*, the reader will discover praying the Scriptures as an important spiritual practice....I am certain that this text will be very useful to young people and adults who wish to learn about Sacred Scripture and the history of Salvation which it makes known to us, as well as the cultural and historical context of its many books."

MOST REVEREND MICHAEL J. BRANSFIELD,
BISHOP OF WHEELING-CHARLESTON

Acknowledgments

BIBLE STUDIES and reflections such as those in this book depend on the help of others who read the manuscript and make suggestions. I am especially indebted to Sister Anne Francis Bartus, CSJ, DMin, whose vast experience and knowledge was very helpful in bringing this series to its final form.

The *Liguori Catholic Bible Study* series is lovingly dedicated to the memory of my parents, Kathleen and Angor Anderson, in gratitude for all they shared with all who knew them, especially with my siblings and me.

Introduction to the
Liguori Catholic Bible Study

READING THE BIBLE can be daunting. It is a complex book, and many a person of good will has begun reading the Bible only to put it down out of utter confusion. Having a companion is a good thing, and the *Liguori Catholic Bible Study* is a solid one at that. Over the course of twenty-one books, it will point out messages and themes, personalities and events. Along the way you'll see how different books of the Bible arose because of the need to address new situations.

Across the centuries people of faith have asked, "Where is God in this moment?" People of faith ask the same question today, and millions of Catholics look to the Bible to encourage them in their journey of faith. Wisdom teaches us not to undertake Bible study alone, disconnected from the Church that has received the Scriptures as a gift to be shared and treasured. When used as a source for prayer and thoughtful reflection, the Bible comes alive.

What you want to get out of Bible study will dictate what method you use in reading the Bible. One goal of the *Liguori Catholic Bible Study* is to give you and other participants greater familiarity with the Bible and its structure, themes, personalities, and message. But that is not enough. An additional goal is to help you know Christ more deeply by praying with Scripture. God's message is as compelling and urgent today as it has been through the centuries, but we only get part of the message if it's memorized and stuck in our heads. God's word is meant for the entire person, physically, emotionally, and spiritually. We are baptized into life with Christ, and we are called to live more fully with Christ today. This is done as we practice the values of justice and peace, forgiveness and community with each other. God's new covenant was written on the hearts of the people of Israel; we, their spiritual descendants, are loved that intimately by God today. The *Liguori Catholic Bible Study* is a way to draw close to God, in whose image and likeness we were fashioned.

Group and Individual Study

The *Liguori Catholic Bible Study* series is intended for group and individual study and prayer. Each lesson contains a section for groups to study, reflect, pray, and share biblical reflections among those gathered. By using the books in this series, anyone should be able to join or even start a study group. Beginning with two or three people gathered together in a home or announcing the meeting of a biblical study group in a parish or community can bring surprising results. Also included in each lesson is a second section for individuals to further study each book of Scripture. Many people want to learn more about the Bible but may not know where to begin. This series hopes to provide that beginning and to ensure its continuation until the participants have become familiar with all the books of the Bible.

Since reading the Bible has as its purpose the deepening of one's relationship with God, the study of the Bible could be a lifelong project, always enriching those who wish to be faithful to God's word. Once people have read, understood, and been enriched by a study of the whole Bible, they may begin again, making new discoveries with each new adventure into a comprehensive understanding of the word of God.

The Living Word of God

While thousands of people of every nation squeezed into Saint Peter's Square when Pope John Paul II lay dying, those closest to the pope gathered around his bed. They all say he was conscious to the end, and that one of his last requests was, "Read the Bible to me." Pope John Paul II faced many challenges in his life, but he built his faith on the words of the Bible and found strength in its message.

Throughout history, the Church has emphasized the importance of becoming familiar with the Bible. In recent times, a love for reading the sacred Scriptures has become evident in the growing number of biblical study groups gathering in parishes and neighborhood communities. In the last half-century, popes have supported and encouraged the reading of the Bible and have given an example of the importance of the Scriptures in their own lives.

In 2008, Pope Benedict XVI convened a gathering of bishops in Rome to discuss the Bible. A gathering of bishops of this type is known as a synod. It consists of bishop representatives from around the world. The pope's primary concern was the challenge of encouraging more Catholics to read the Bible. He instructed the synod's planners to stress that acts of reading, interpreting, and living the words of Scripture are fundamental to the faith life of Christians. The pope said the Bible cannot be thought of as a message of the past but should be read as the living word of God and a challenge for all people today. He declared it is essential for every Christian to develop a personal relationship with the word of the Lord.

Pope Benedict believes the Bible must be seen in its totality as the living word of God. This series will address the entire Old and New Testaments, knowing that the full meaning of the word of God can be grasped only through a total understanding of the books as they relate one to the other. Pope Benedict added that the Bible belongs to the people, not the scholars. This series approaches the study of the Bible as a spiritual adventure, one that attempts to present biblical texts in a readable and understandable format while at the same time treating the Bible with deep respect as the living and inspiring word of God.

One of Pope Benedict's primary convictions is that the New Testament offers the key to understanding the Old Testament and that, as a whole, the Bible necessarily leads to Christ.

Lectio Divina
(Sacred Reading)

A BIBLE STUDY is not just a matter of gaining an intellectual knowledge of the Bible but also a matter of gaining a greater understanding of God's love and concern for creation. The purpose of reading and knowing the Bible is to enrich one's relationship with God. God loves us and gave us the Bible to illustrate that love. As Pope Benedict reminds us, a study of the Bible is not only an intellectual pursuit but also a spiritual adventure that should influence us in our dealings with God and neighbor.

The Meaning of *Lectio Divina*

Lectio divina is a Latin expression meaning divine or sacred reading. Many clergy, religious, and laity use this process for their daily spiritual reading, which has as its aim to develop a closer and more loving relationship with God. The *lectio divina* process consists of Scripture readings, reflection, and prayer. It is not only a time for sacred reading but also a time for sacred reflection. Learning about the Scriptures has as its purpose the living of its message, acts that demand a period of reflection on the Scripture passages. This text provides for that period of reflection.

The Role of Prayer in Divine Reading *(Lectio Divina)*

Prayer is a necessary element for the practice of *lectio divina*. The entire process of reading and reflecting is a prayer. It is not merely an intellectual pursuit but a spiritual one. The next books in this series will include prayers that may be used privately or in a group. Some people may wish to keep a journal of their daily meditations.

Pondering the Word of God

Lectio divina is the ancient Christian spiritual practice of reading the holy Scriptures with intentionality and devotion. This practice helps Christians center themselves and descend to the level of the heart to enter an inner-focused quiet space, finding God.

This sacred reading is distinct from other types of reading to obtain knowledge or information. Furthermore, *lectio divina* is more than the pious practice of spiritual reading. Rather, it is the practice of opening ourselves to the action and inspiration of the Holy Spirit. As we intentionally focus our attentiveness and become present to the inner meaning of the scriptural text we are reading, the Holy Spirit enlightens our minds and hearts. We come to the text willing to be influenced by a deeper meaning that lies within the words and thoughts we ponder.

In this space we open ourselves to be challenged and changed by the inner meaning we experience. We approach the text in a spirit of faith and obedience as a disciple ready to be taught by the Holy Spirit. As we savor the sacred text, we let go of our usual control of how we expect God to act in our lives and surrender our hearts and consciences to the flow of the divine (*divina*) through sacred reading (*lectio*).

The fundamental principle of *lectio divina* leads us to understand the profound mystery of the Incarnation: "The Word became flesh" not only in history but also within us.

Praying *Lectio* Today

The practice of *lectio divina* is simple and easy to follow. Four actions are practiced in this ancient tradition.

First, we read a passage from the Scriptures. This is known as *"lectio."* The word of God is read aloud, and the hearers listen attentively to the spoken word.

Second, the selected passage is prayed with attention as we listen for some specific meaning that comes to mind. The reading is silently reflected upon, which is known as *"meditatio."*

Third, the exercise becomes active. Pick a word, sentence, or idea that surfaces from your consideration of the chosen text. Is the reading reminding you of a person, place, or experience? If so, pray about it. Compose your thoughts and reflection into a simple word or phrase. This activity is called *"oratio."*

Finally, quiet yourself and let your thoughts, feelings, and concerns fade away as you consider the selected passage in the previous step (*oratio*). If you are distracted, use your prayer word to help your return to silence. This is *"contemplatio."* The Scripture is transformed in our hearing as we pray and allow our hearts to unite intimately with the Lord.

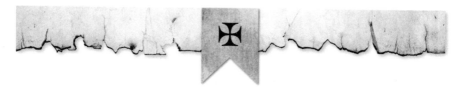

Understanding the Background of the Bible

IN USING THE BIBLE AS A GUIDE, it is important to understand what the authors are telling us. The authors and editors had a specific purpose in mind when they wrote and edited the Scriptures. By studying the background of the Bible writers, their period in history, and the political and religious situations in which they found themselves, we can gain an insight into the meaning of the Bible text. Misinterpretation of the biblical texts has led to some tragic mistakes in past and recent history. The Bible has God as its central focus, and it enables us to examine our actions and decisions in relationship to this focus.

Although most readers are anxious to begin with specific books of the Bible, an overview of the Bible such as that found in this book can be most helpful in placing the books of the Bible in their proper context. An overview of Old Testament history and writings will enable the reader to better understand each book being studied in the total context of the Bible. The overview of the whole Bible in *Introduction to the Bible* will also provide a helpful resource when the study group or individual moves on to each book.

CHAPTER ONE

The Bible

I. IDENTIFYING THE INSPIRED BOOKS

On a Sabbath day in Nazareth, Jesus, as a dedicated and pious Jew who worshiped in the synagogue every Sabbath, entered the synagogue to worship with the Jewish community. The worship leader invited Jesus to read the Scripture for the day. Jesus opened the scroll and read a passage from Isaiah the prophet that began with the words: "The Spirit of the Lord is upon me" (Luke 4:18). In Luke's Gospel, Jesus' public mission to the crowds began with the words that follow. As he rolled up the scroll, he declared, "Today this Scripture passage is fulfilled in your hearing" (Luke 4:21).

As we approach our study, we know the Bible is the inspired message of God. We refer to the words of the Bible as the word of God. If we approach the Bible with faith that we are reading the word of God, then we can say with Jesus, "The Spirit of the Lord is upon me." It is only under the inspiration of the Holy Spirit that we are able to read the Bible with faith. Faith comes to us as a gift of the Holy Spirit. God speaks and we listen. When we allow the words of the Bible to shape our lives, we can say with Jesus, "Today this Scripture passage is fulfilled in your hearing."

A Library Under One Roof

An English literature student learning about the classical literature of the twentieth century purchased a book required for class work that contained sample writings from twentieth-century authors. Between the covers of this sizable book were poems, short stories, essays, articles, biographies, historical excerpts, and commentaries about each author whose work appeared in the book. A number of editors worked on bringing this book together under one cover. When the student saw the size of the book and reviewed its contents, he remarked to his classmates, "This is not just a book! This is a whole library!"

Welcome to the Bible. Like the literature book mentioned in this opening story, the Bible is not a single book but a whole library of writings from various authors from different backgrounds and various periods of history.

The Word "Bible" Tells It All

"Bible" is essentially a one-word description of the book's contents. The word has its origin in the Greek word *biblion,* which means "papyrus," "scroll," or "little book." The plural use of the Greek word *biblia,* meaning "scrolls," or "little books," comes closer to the name and content of the Bible. The word originates from the Phoenician city of Byblos, where the inhabitants cut papyrus into strips that were dried and used for writing purposes.

The writings of the Bible consist of histories, poetry, wise sayings, prophecies, hymns, personal letters, liturgical prayers, and a number of other diverse types of writing, written over a period of many centuries. The authors of the books of the Bible included farmers, shepherds, kings, priests, prophets, warriors, and slaves. Some were exemplary lovers of God, while others had great difficulty in remaining faithful to the one true God. Like the editors of the student's book about twentieth-century literature, the editors of the Bible brought the various writings together under one cover.

The Unknown Authors

Most of the writers of the Bible did not identify themselves. Their purpose was to share a message, not themselves. Later traditions identified certain significant manuscripts in the Bible as being written by some well-known people in Israel history. Some of the books attributed to famous prophets, for instance, may have been spoken by these prophets and passed on orally until someone wrote them down and credited them to the prophet who first spoke them. Tradition sometimes attributed to a book the name of an author who was not the actual scribe. For instance, many commentators believed Moses wrote the first five books of the Bible, but the books contain some instructions for life in the Promised Land that could only have developed after the Hebrew people settled there. Moses may have written some aspects of the story within the first five books, but he most likely was not the author of the final text.

And in the New Testament, some authors did not identify themselves, although later tradition—correctly or incorrectly—attributed certain names to specific books or letters. Some writers would choose the name of a well-known apostle to give the book credence, or they would choose the name because they believed they were passing on the true teaching of that apostle. The Apostle Paul was clearly the author of some of the New Testament letters attributed to him, since he identifies himself at the beginning of several of his letters as the author. On the other hand, he didn't write some of the letters attributed to him.

Revelation

We can know some things about God through our human experiences, but there are other things we cannot know about God unless he reveals them to us. By looking at the beauty of nature, we can experience some idea of God's sense of beauty, but the human mind can never experience the magnitude of God. Everything we experience is like a wisp of smoke in the blazing beauty of God. We need revelation to know about God's dealings with creation. The word of God that comes to us in the Bible is a great gift from God. Jeremiah says, "When I found your words, I devoured them; your words were my joy, the happiness of my heart" (Jeremiah 15:16).

The Message of Revelation

We believe God loves us, that God forgives us when we sincerely seek forgiveness, and that God has concern for all of creation. We believe that human beings are the peak of God's creation and that we will be raised from the dead and live in eternity. We believe all of these ideas about God and creation, but we need revelation to support these beliefs. When we read the inspired word of God, we have the security of knowing that God does indeed love us and has concern for us.

Revelation, however, goes a step further. Revelation reveals to us some deep mysteries about God. It reveals that Jesus and the Holy Spirit are one with God the Father. When we speak of mystery in the Scriptures, we are not using the word in the sense of a murder mystery or some similar sense, but we are using it in the sense of something unknown and not able to be understood with our human mind. Since mystery in this sense is beyond our human ability of understanding, revelation is the only way we can know about it. Even though God has revealed it, understanding it is still a mystery. Mysteries are also different from problems. If I owe someone five dollars, I solve my problem by paying my debt. Understanding myself or someone else may be an attempt to solve a mystery. We sometimes hear the expression, "It is a mystery to me why he acts that way." In this case, we are not trying to solve a problem alone but seeking to understand someone.

Although God is pure spirit and neither male nor female, the members of the early Church followed the trends of their own time and culture, which centered on the male. It was a patriarchal society. In the culture of Jesus' day, they would mostly choose the male image of Father as the parent image for God, although there are some hints in the Bible of a feminine side of God. Isaiah the prophet portrays God as speaking to those inhabiting Jerusalem and writes: "As a mother comforts her child, so will I comfort you" (Isaiah 66:13). Jesus uses a similar image of comfort for the people of Jerusalem when he laments over Jerusalem, saying, "I yearned to gather your children together, as a hen gathers her young under her wings, but you were unwilling" (Matthew 23:37). Since the New Testament had to make a distinction between the first and second person of God, the title "Father" is used far more often for God in the New Testament than in the Old Testament. The people of the Old Testament had no idea of the Trinity.

Public revelation ended with the last book accepted into the Bible. We no longer have public revelation, which means a revelation given to a community and declared inspired by the authority of that community. If a person has a vision of God and tells us that God expects us to pray a certain prayer each day, we have no obligation to follow such a revelation. Private visions may bring a revelation for the person who receives it, but it is not public revelation. We are not obliged to follow it as the word of God for us. The truth of private revelation must also be tested against public revelation. If someone claims that God has revealed something that is contrary to public revelation, we must reject the so-called revelation as false.

The Inspired Authors

When the authors wrote the manuscripts accepted as inspired in the Bible, they had no idea that they were writing sacred Scripture. God did not lean over their shoulder and whisper, "Take a message!" The writers wrote according to their style, their historical circumstance, and their openness to the inspiration of God. Some authors of the Bible claimed that God spoke to them directly or through a heavenly messenger, while others claimed they had thoroughly investigated what they heard passed on to them by the community. It was up to religious authorities to determine which books belonged in the Bible.

The Canon (Guiding Rule) of the Sacred Scriptures

"Canon," a Greek word, refers to a rod or rule used for measuring. The use of the word "canon" for the books of the Bible provides a measuring rod to determine which books belong to the Scriptures. The measuring rod for the Bible depended on the reverence and usage given by the community to certain religious manuscripts. A specific religious authority investigated the community usage of particular books and determined which books or manuscripts were to be accepted as inspired.

During Old Testament times and into the New Testament period, there were a number of manuscripts about God's dealings with his people. Some were confirmed as belonging to the canon of the inspired Scriptures, others were not. Declaring which manuscripts belonged to the canon of the Scriptures guided the faithful about the inspired word of God. In short, the Bible is a collection of the books and manuscripts that religious authorities determined to be inspired.

The Language of the Books of the Old Testament

Since the original authors of the Old Testament were Hebrews, the largest portion of the Old Testament was written in the Hebrew language or an Aramaic dialect closely related to Hebrew. All the books and manuscripts in the Bible existed for a long period of time before editors gathered them into a single collection. The identification of which books belonged in the Bible had to wait until a later date.

In the sixth and fifth centuries before Christ, the writings of the Old Testament were gathered together, comprising only books written in Hebrew. Still, at that time, there were no official statements declaring they belonged to sacred Scripture, but the Hebrew people accepted them as central to their worship and way of life. The people of Israel had commonly accepted some readings, hymns, laws, and forms of worship as inspired, believing that they came directly from the words of God, such as the commandments God gave to Moses.

When Alexander the Great conquered a large portion of the known world in the fourth century before Christ, he spread the Greek language and culture throughout his empire. The Israelites who lived outside Palestine became assimilated into Greek culture while preserving their Jewish beliefs and practices. The mixture of Greek culture with other cultures came to be known as Hellenism. Some commentators referred to those Jews who lived outside of Palestine and who assimilated some aspects of Greek culture as Hellenistic Jews. Many of them could no longer speak Hebrew. This caused a problem for those who wished to remain faithful to the history and customs of Judaism as found in the sacred Scriptures.

With the loss of the ability to speak Hebrew, it became apparent that a translation of the Hebrew Scriptures into Greek was necessary. This translation began around 250 years before the birth of Jesus. The work eventually gained the name of the Septuagint, Greek for "seventy." Tradition says that seventy-two scholars, working independently of each other, arrived at the exact same translation. This legend naturally led to the conclusion that God had guided this work and that it was authentic. The Septuagint added a number of Jewish historical and religious writings that were not part of the original Hebrew Bible and which, although held in high esteem, were judged by Jewish scholars ninety years after the birth of Jesus as not belonging to the inspired Hebrew Scriptures. Greek-speaking Christians, however, accepted these writings as inspired and therefore belonging in the Bible.

The Language of the Books of the New Testament

Many of the authors of the New Testament wrote their manuscripts mostly in the Greek language commonly used in their day. This made the Greek Septuagint an important source of Old Testament Scriptures for the writers of the New Testament. The New Testament includes many clear references to the Old Testament and a number of subtle and obscure references often missed by the ordinary reader. The value of commentaries on the New Testament books is that they can uncover some of these obscure messages.

The Apocrypha and Deuterocanonical Books

In relation to the issue of the books of the Bible not written in Hebrew, the word "apocrypha" ("hidden") was first used by Saint Jerome when he translated the Bible into Latin. His translation is known as the Latin Vulgate. Apocrypha may have indicated that certain writings would remain hidden or not understood by the uneducated reader. Jerome did consider the books found only in Greek in high esteem when he included them in his translation, although he did not specifically include them in the inspired Scriptures.

The Protestant Reformation in the sixteenth century eventually led most Protestant Christians to refuse to accept the apocrypha as belonging to the inspired Scriptures, since many believed that only the Hebrew writings of the Old Testament truly demonstrated the faith of Israel. The Church's Council of Trent declared in 1546 that these books were deuterocanonical (doo-ter-oh-can-ON-i-cal), which meant they belonged to a second canon of sacred Scripture, which also meant they were held by Catholics to be the inspired word of God and worthy of being read during worship. The term "protocanonical," which means the first canon, is used to designate the books found in the Hebrew Bible, and deuterocanoncal refers to manuscripts found in the Greek Septuagint translation. The writers of the New Testament depended on the Greek Septuagint translation of the Old Testament, which contained books that would later be referred to by most Protestants as the apocrypha.

Some editions of the Bible include text from both deuterocanonical and noncanonical Scriptures in a single section designated "Apocrypha." This arrangement can lead to confusion between the otherwise distinct terms "deuterocanonical" and "apocryphal." Some books read in the early Church period by some members of the Church were not accepted as canonical and are termed apocryphal by the Roman Catholic Church. These books are often included under the heading of apocrypha in Protestant translations.

The deuterocanonical books—known as the apocrypha in Protestant Bibles—are Tobit, Judith, the Wisdom of Solomon, Sirach (Ecclesiasticus), Baruch (including the epistle of Jeremiah), 1 and 2 Maccabees, and additions to the Books of Esther and Daniel, such as the Prayer of the Three Hebrew Children, Susanna, and Bel and the Dragon.

The Number of Books in the Bible

The Roman Catholic Church and Eastern Christianity include seventy-three books in their Bible, while Protestants include sixty-six books in their Bible. As mentioned above, most Protestant denominations do not accept the deuterocanonical books in their Bible. As a result, the Old Testament texts accepted as inspired by the Roman Catholic Church and Eastern Christianity contain forty-six books, while most Protestant

OT NT

P 39 27

Bibles contain thirty-nine books in the Old Testament. All of Christianity in general accepts the twenty-seven books of the New Testament as the inspired word of God.

C 46 27

Review

✠ What do we mean by the canon of the Scriptures?

✠ What languages are the source languages of the Old and New Testaments?

✠ What do commentators mean when they speak of the "apocrypha?"

✠ How many books are contained in the Protestant and Roman Catholic Bibles?

Reflection

✠ The canonicity of the Bible tells us which writings are accepted as inspired. How can this help you in reading the Bible?

✠ The Old and New Testaments speak of God's dealing with people from ancient times to the present. What can the reading of the Bible teach you about God?

II. COVENANT (TESTAMENT)

The Gospel of Luke tells us that Jesus, at the Last Supper, took bread, blessed it, broke it, and gave it to his disciples, saying, "This is my body, which will be given for you; do this in memory of me"(Luke 22:19). He then took the cup and said, "This cup is the new covenant in my blood, which will be shed for you" (Luke 22:20). With this, the Christian covenant with God began, a covenant sealed by the Body and Blood of Jesus.

A Story of Covenants

The story of the Bible is a story of covenants made, covenants broken, covenants renewed, and a new covenant of Christ's Body and Blood. The central component of the Bible is the covenant. In the Bible, a covenant designates a relationship and agreement based upon shared commitments that normally entail promises, commitments, and rituals. "Testament" and "covenant" can be used interchangeably. A covenant may involve a situation where a superior party establishes the terms of an agreement and a lesser party who agrees to obey this authority, or an agreement between equals who are mutually compelled to observe its stipulations.

The Old Covenant (Testament)

In the Hebrew Bible, God initiates a covenant with Israel. God, in this case, is the superior party who establishes the terms of a covenant with the lesser party, namely the human beings he created. There are several covenants between God and the Israelites in the Old Testament. A major covenant of the Old Testament took place on Mount Sinai where the one true God promises to be the God of the Hebrews, and they vow to obey him. Because God mediates the covenant through Moses, it is called the Mosaic covenant. It is also referred to as the Sinai covenant, since it was given to Moses on Mount Sinai. In breaking a covenant, the people would sin seriously and incur God's wrath. The people believed that when the nation broke its covenant with God, God would punish them, not to destroy them but to cleanse them and bring them back to living in accord with the precepts of the covenant. No matter how many times or how gravely the people break a covenant with God, God will always remain faithful to the promises of the covenant and wait for the nation to repent and become faithful to the covenant once again.

The New Covenant (Testament)

Because of the sinfulness of the Judeans, Jeremiah predicted that God would make a new covenant with God's people. For Christians, the Mosaic covenant came to be known as the Old Covenant, and the covenant given by Jesus became known as the New Covenant. Since the word also means "testament," this naturally led to the covenants receiving the titles "Old Testament" and "New Testament." To Jews, of course, there is no Old Testament, since they do not accept the New Testament of Jesus

Christ. To Jews, the Mosaic covenant is as relevant today as it was when Moses received it.

Some, in consideration of the sensitivities of the Jewish people, attempt to refer to the Old Testament as the "Hebrew Scriptures" and to the New Testament as the "Christian Scriptures," but in light of what has been said about the deuterocanonical books in the Catholic New Testament, Catholics cannot refer to the whole Old Testament as the Hebrew Bible, since Catholics accept certain books as canonical that Jewish scholars rejected ninety years after the birth of Jesus.

The Size of the Old and New Testaments

The Old Testament is three times longer than the Christian Scriptures because it covers more time. The Old Testament tells of God's dealings with the people of Israel for about 1,500 years. The New Testament covers less than a hundred years and speaks of God's dealings with the people through Jesus Christ, his teachings, and the application of his message to life after his resurrection. For the Christian, however, the Christian Scriptures (the New Testament) are far more important than the Hebrew Scriptures (the Old Testament). The New Testament tells the Christian how he or she should respond to the fact that Jesus Christ, the Son of God, became human, died, and rose for us. Without the message of the New Testament, Christianity would not exist. We Christians live in the New Testament era.

The Importance of the Old Testament to Christians

Judaism and Christianity are historical religions. The history of the Jewish people is a history of God's activity among the Chosen People of Israel. The history of Christianity is a continuation of God's activity in the world through the person of Jesus Christ, the Son of God. Jesus himself was a Jew who cherished the history of the Hebrew nation from the beginning of creation to his own lifetime. Since Christianity centers its faith on Jesus the Christ, it is important to understand the biblical stories, prophecies, and wisdom that influenced his life and message.

Jesus Came to Fulfill the Law

The Christian who reads the message of the Hebrew Scriptures actually approaches it in a different manner than the Jewish reader who does not accept that Jesus is the Christ. For Christians, the Hebrew Scriptures reached their fulfillment in Jesus, the long-awaited Christ who arrived and brought a new meaning to the Hebrew Scriptures. The believing Jew reads the Hebrew Scriptures with a view to some fulfillment yet to take place. Jesus himself told his followers that he did not come to destroy the law but to bring it to fulfillment. For Christians and Jews alike, the Hebrew Scriptures bring spiritual nourishment and insight. A study of the Old Testament for Christians brings a deeper understanding of the New Testament and an insight into understanding the person of Jesus, who was a good and dedicated Jew.

The Dead Sea Scrolls

Until 1947, the oldest known copies of the Hebrew Scriptures were referred to as the Masoretic Texts, which dated to the ninth and tenth centuries after the birth of Jesus. One day, a Bedouin boy, while tending his flock of sheep, threw a stone into a cave at Qumran on the northwest shore of the Dead Sea and heard pottery shattering inside. His random tossing of a stone into a cave had an astounding impact on Scripture studies. Upon investigation, he found clay jars containing leather scrolls hidden in the cave. Scholars later examined the site and discovered almost a thousand manuscripts from the Hebrew Bible. Other texts found in the caves disclosed the existence of a monastic type of life for a group known as the Essenes. Researchers believe the scrolls may have been copied by members of the Essene community.

The value of the discovery is that the scrolls include the oldest known surviving copies of biblical and extra-biblical documents. The discovery provided an entire library of religious manuscripts dating from about two centuries before Jesus to a century and a half after. The boy's random throw led to uncovering a cache of biblical manuscripts and other ancient writings stored in ceramic pots more than 2,000 years ago. Besides the abundance of helpful knowledge gained from these manuscripts, the texts verified the reliability of some ancient writings of the Scriptures. Many of them were fragments of Old Testament manuscripts along with some commentaries about the texts. Many included a number of discrepancies found in later copies, but lengthy sections of the Book of Isaiah had little significant change.

The precious finding received the name "Dead Sea Scrolls" because Qumran is near the Dead Sea, which is a little less than 1,300 feet below sea level. The Dead Sea received its name from its large concentration of salt, which makes it impossible for anything to live in the sea. The salt is so dense that people can easily float on its surface. Today, the area is a resort for many who believe that its waters refresh one's physical and mental health.

The Bible as a Religious Book

In the seventeenth century, the scientist Galileo was condemned to house arrest because he declared that the sun was the center of the universe. Those who condemned him said, among other accusations, that he was teaching lessons contrary to the Scriptures. At the time, many believed the earth was the center of the universe because the Scriptures spoke of the sun, not the earth, standing still. The Bible tells us that, in one of Joshua's battles, he prayed that the sun would stand still: And "the sun stood still" (Joshua 10:13). Recent popes recognize that Galileo, instead of being a heretic or teaching false information contrary to the Scriptures, was correct about his scientific theories.

In Galileo's era, people misunderstood the type of literature used in the Bible. The Bible is a religious book, not a scientific or historical one. The Bible teaches salvation history, which involves God's dealings with his people. Current scholars all agree that the Bible does not intend to make scientific statements or relate exact history. This does not mean there is no history in the Bible, but to understand the Bible, the reader must understand its purpose and the cultural mentality of those who composed the books in it. The reader must also understand that those who composed the Bible had the commonly held world view of their day, which held that the earth was flat and the sun, moon, and stars rode on a kind of large dome in the sky, moving from one end of the earth to the other in the course of a day.

Inerrancy in the Bible

Jews and Christians alike believe the Bible, as inspired, is free from religious error. As mentioned above, the Bible is not a scientific book, nor does it always present accurate history. It is a religious book with a religious message. This, however, must also be understood: There are some messages in the Bible that are not supported when compared to the Bible's total teaching. For instance, the Book of Job speaks of the grave as being the end of one's existence, but later in time, authors taught about resurrection from the dead. When the Sadducees of Jesus' day challenge Jesus' message about resurrection and declare that it is not found in the Torah, they are expressing a belief held by many pious Jews. Belief in life after death began about 150 years before Jesus' birth.

The reality that some parts of the Bible may seem to be in error points to the human element of revelation, which works two ways. It involves divine inspiration, but it also involves the writer, the one who receives this inspiration. Every biblical passage must be in agreement with the total teaching of the Bible in order to be accepted as free from error.

Religion and Life

The writers of the Bible also lived in a world where there was little or no separation of religion from the daily rituals of life. Their eras differed from ours. Pagans believed in many gods, while Jews and Christians of the biblical era believed in the one true God. In contrast to the modern era, there were no atheists. For Jews and pagans alike, everything that happened was related to a divine being. Some believed the gods caused storms, famines, plagues, and a number of challenging aspects to life. Jews and Christians, however, realized that the false gods were not gods at all. They did not exist. The one true God was the one who controlled creation and guided and protected them. In refusing to believe in many gods and keeping faith in the one true God, even in the midst of trials, Jews and Christians were unique in their world. Their history was a religious history, a true history of salvation. Their God was with them in good times and in bad.

In reading the Old Testament, one must beware of viewing God as stern or wrathful. We read that the God of the Israelites punished the Chosen People, not to destroy them but to help them recognize their need to be faithful to the covenant. God admonished them, supported them, punished them, led them in battle, parted the sea for them, and loved them. There are a number of passages that present God as compassionate and loving, one who longs to take the people and embrace them as a mother hugs a child.

For Christians, the Bible is a long journey that reaches its fulfillment when the "word became flesh and dwelt among us." The Son of God came into the world to bring us salvation that came as a result of his passion, death, and resurrection. That is really what the Bible is all about: God's desire is that we worship the one true and loving God, and that we love as Jesus did.

Translations of the Bible

A trip to a bookstore will soon reveal to the seeker of a good translation of the Bible that the shelves contain many translations, leaving the reader to wonder which is the best translation and why there are so many. At various periods of history, scholars have translated the Bible into practically every known language. The reason for different translations in English is that the understanding of certain words change. For instance, when the older Roman Catholic Bibles were translated, people used "thee" and "thou" for "you" in daily conversation. As a result, the translations of Catholic and Protestant Bibles had Jesus using "thee, thou," and other words of old English spoken at the time of the translations. The original authors of the Bible manuscripts wrote in the common language of the people of their day. Today's translators use the vocabulary and idioms of everyday speech found in modern society. Added to this is the fact that scholars have discovered more exact translations of certain words used in the original manuscripts.

For Roman Catholics, the translation proclaimed from the pulpit is from the *New American Bible*, whose revision was completed in 2010. The title page of the *New American Bible* says the book was "translated from the original languages with critical use of all the ancient sources." It is a scholarly and more easily understood presentation of the biblical manuscripts.

Review

✠ What does the word "Bible" tell us about its contents?

✠ What is the value of the Dead Sea Scrolls, and where did they get their name?

✠ What is the importance of knowing that the Bible is basically a religious book with a religious message?

✠ What do we mean when we say that religion and life were one in ancient Israel?

Reflection

✠ Jesus gave us a new covenant in the Eucharist. When you celebrate the Eucharist, are you aware that you are recommitting yourself to a new covenant with Christ?

✠ The Bible is a religious book. What are some spiritual messages you can recall from reading the Bible or listening to the Bible being read?

CHAPTER TWO

History Before the Exile

I. THE PENTATEUCH (TORAH)

The Israelites believed God spoke to them through the mediation of Moses and the prophets. They recognized that God was a loving God who not only protected the nation but gave them a law that enabled them to show their love for God. The law was not only a list of what the Israelites should do, but it was also a story of God's dealings with the chosen family of Abraham. God was the one true God who journeyed with them, became angry with them when they did not remain faithful to the law, and miraculously protected them when all human endeavors failed. The first five books of the Bible became their sacred law, their sign that God was with them and their guiding light enabling them to show their respect and love for the God who loved them.

The first five books of the Bible (Genesis, Exodus, Leviticus, Numbers, and Deuteronomy) form the Pentateuch, a word that comes from the Greek for "five books." Jewish tradition refers to the first five books as the "Torah," meaning "teaching" or "law." The books center on the Sinai covenant made through the human mediation of Moses with God on behalf of the Hebrew nation. In the Hebrew Scriptures the books are referred to by their opening words, while in Christian translations they are named according to their content. The collected books are the result of the writings of various authors. Even within a single book, one may find several different collections written by different authors.

The Book of Genesis

The first book of the Pentateuch is Genesis, which covers the period from the creation of the world to the settlement of the family of Jacob in Egypt. Most commentators refer to this time of history as the Prehistoric Period.

Creation

According to Genesis, God created the world in six days and rested on the seventh day. Jews of Jesus' day (and many today) viewed the seventh-day rest (the Sabbath) as a strict rule. The Bible tells us: "God blessed the seventh day and made it holy, because on it he rested from all the work he had done in creation" (Genesis 2:3). Most Scripture scholars consider the story of creation to be a myth that has some similarities to the more ancient Mesopotamian myths about creation. As with other books in the Bible, the creation story presents an inspired religious message about God, even if the science and history did not happen as presented. The inspired message speaks of a God of order who created the world out of nothing and created human beings as the peak of creation, making the union of man and woman so sacred that, in God's eyes, "the two shall become one." The Book of Genesis names Adam and Eve as the first man and woman God created.

Sin Gains a Grip on the World

The Book of Genesis continues with the story of sin gaining a grip on God's world. Adam and Eve sin and are cast out of the Garden of Eden. Cain kills Abel, and other sins follow until the world becomes so depraved that God tries a new creation by sending a Flood and saving only Noah and his family. After the Flood, one of Noah's sons, Ham, sins by ridiculing his father (an atrocious sin in Israelite families) and is exiled. Soon, people seek their own way to heaven, symbolized by the building of the tower of Babel. God then mixes up languages so people can no longer communicate with each other.

The Family of Abraham

At this point, Abraham arrives on the scene. He is most likely the first historical character in the Old Testament, although many of the stories told about him have been passed on by word of mouth for such a long period of time that many of them have been greatly embellished and lack precision. God enters into a covenant with Abraham by which God promises that Abraham will be the father of a host of nations and that the whole land of Canaan (Palestine) will be given to Abraham and his descendants. The one true God is to be the God of Abraham and his descendants, and the sign of the covenant is the circumcision of all male children. Less than a year later, Abraham and Sarah give birth to a son they name Isaac. God challenges Abraham's faith by ordering him to sacrifice Isaac. As Abraham is about to sacrifice his son, God orders him not to lay a hand on the child. Because of Abraham's faith, God renews the promise of making Abraham the father of a great nation.

Isaac becomes the father of Esau and Jacob. Esau is the firstborn with the right of inheriting the promise made to Abraham, but Jacob and his mother trick Isaac, who has become blind in his old age, and Isaac blesses Jacob, thinking he was blessing Esau. Jacob flees from Esau, finds work with the family of his cousin, Laban, and in time becomes the father of twelve sons. Jacob decides to return home, but he first sends gifts to Esau with the hope that Esau will receive him back. Not knowing what Esau would do, Jacob sends his family to safety across the river and awaits Esau alone. That night, an angel wrestles him until dawn. At dawn, the angel asks Jacob his name. When he answers that it is Jacob, the angel changes Jacob's name to Israel, which refers to Jacob's competing with divine beings.

Jacob's Family in Egypt

Eleven of Jacob's sons become jealous of their brother, Joseph, who is a dreamer. Joseph dreams of his brothers bowing down before him. The brothers eventually sell Joseph to merchants on their way to Egypt. In Egypt, Joseph is falsely accused of seducing the wife of a nobleman who owns Joseph as a slave, and he casts Joseph into prison. In time, the Pharaoh has a dream, and Joseph interprets the Pharaoh's dream to mean that the land would have seven years of plenty and seven years of famine. The Pharaoh puts Joseph in charge of storing goods during the first seven years and distributing them during the second seven years. Joseph becomes so powerful in Egypt that he is able to invite the families of his brothers into Egypt. Jacob dies in Egypt. Joseph also dies in Egypt, with the wish that his bones be moved to the Promised Land. The Book of Genesis, having explained how the tribes of Israel ended up in Egypt, ends with Joseph's death.

Although the Book of Genesis explains the origin of the world and the origins of the Chosen People, it is the covenant God made with Abraham that is pivotal to the book. Jesus will refer to the people of his own era and nationality as the children of Abraham.

The Book of Exodus

Four hundred years elapse between the end of Genesis and the beginning of Exodus. An Egyptian Pharaoh, knowing nothing about Joseph and how the Hebrew tribes came into Egypt, feared that the rapid growth of the Hebrew people would overrun the land. He ordered that all newborn boys be thrown into the Nile River and drowned, but Moses' sister sets him adrift on the river. Pharaoh's daughter finds him, gives him the name Moses, and raises him.

Moses Leads the People Out of Egypt

As an adult, Moses kills an Egyptian who is beating an Israelite slave and flees. He marries and becomes a sheepherder. One day, while tending his father-in-law's flock, Moses encounters God, who appears in a burning bush. When he asks God's name, God replies, "I AM WHO I AM." At God's direction, Moses returns to Egypt and informs the Pharaoh of God's demand to let the Hebrews leave. When Pharaoh refuses God's request, God sends ten plagues. With the tenth plague, God instructs Moses to have the people kill a lamb and paint the blood of the lamb on the Hebrews' doorposts.

They are to eat the lamb like a people ready to take a trip. When the night came, Moses and the people celebrated the first Passover. The firstborn of all the people and animals not having the blood on their doorposts died.

At the death of the firstborn, the Pharaoh allows the Hebrews to leave Egypt with their flocks and herds, but then he has second thoughts and goes after them. Miraculously, the Hebrew people pass through the Reed Sea, which parts when Moses raises his staff. When the Egyptians try to use the same path after the Hebrew people reach the other side, the waters return and drown the soldiers.

The Sinai Covenant

The desert journey becomes difficult for the Hebrews, and they complain to Moses, claiming that life was better in Egypt than in the desert. God feeds them with manna in the desert and provides water for them, but they still sin against God. Moses meets God on the mountain, where God proclaims the Covenant Code, which detailed ritual and civil law. Later, after several visits with God, God calls Moses up the mountain to receive a set of stone tablets containing the law. God instructs Moses concerning the construction of the tabernacle where God will dwell permanently among the Chosen People. God gives Moses other instructions on such topics as priestly vestments, the altar and its appointments, and the daily sacrifices to be offered. Aaron becomes the first high priest; the line of Aaron will be the priestly line.

While Moses visits with God on the mountain, the people construct a golden calf as an image of God. Because of this grievous sin of making a false image of God, God threatens to kill all the people, but God relents when Moses begs God not to destroy the people. When Moses comes down the mountain, he angrily smashes the stone tablets and commands the Levites to slaughter the unfaithful Israelites. Later, following a command from God, Moses makes two new tablets on which he writes the words that were on the first tablets. When Moses descends from the mountain after receiving the commandments anew, his face shines so brightly that he must veil his face from the people.

The Sinai covenant is the centerpiece of the Book of Exodus and the

Pentateuch. Some of the laws and directives found in Exodus come from a later era when the people were already settled in the Promised Land. A later editor placed them in Exodus as though they came from God on Mount Sinai.

The Book of Leviticus

The title of "Leviticus" refers to the Levites, the priestly tribe of Israel. Although it bears a name linked with the tribe of Levi, it is not a book just for the priests of Israel but has many portions pertaining to the laity.

The instructions in the Book of Leviticus provide lessons and laws for relating to the holy God. The central idea of Leviticus rests in the words, "Be holy, for I, the LORD your God, am holy." It offers guidance for people who are recognized as sinful yet a people whom God is willing to redeem. Sin can be atoned for through the offering of suitable sacrifices. Although Leviticus recognizes that creation is capable of sin, it also believes that the world retains the capacity for goodness that was present at the beginning of creation. Parts of the book pertain to sacrificial and other ritual laws prescribed for the Levites.

Most scholars agree that the book had an extensive period of growth and that it achieved its present structure in the Persian period (538–332 BC). Leviticus, which contains mostly legislation, interrupts the narrative flow found in the first two books of the Bible.

The Book of Numbers

The Book of Numbers resumes the narrative of the Hebrews' journey through the desert. It begins with a census and offering of gifts on the occasion of the dedication of the tabernacle. Having begun with this encampment of the people at Sinai, the narrative continues as the people move away from Sinai and ends with the Hebrew people settling in the plains of Moab, which is on the east side of the Jordan River. God declared that the generation that left Egypt at the beginning of the exodus journey would not enter the Promised Land because of their lack of trust in God's protection. By the end of the book, this prediction reaches its fulfillment, with a new generation born in the desert ready to enter the Promised Land.

The Book of Deuteronomy

The fifth and last book of the Torah, the Book of Deuteronomy, comes from a word that means "second law." The term could be deceptive, since it does not really contain a new law but a final and partial explanation and fulfillment of the law Moses proclaimed on Sinai. The book contains a replication of the historical events found in other parts of the Pentateuch. It includes a chain of Mosaic discourses by which Moses motivates the people to recall their earlier glory and to look to God's promise of a future conquest. Moses also reminds the people that God has a claim to their trustworthy obedience and love. The final verses of the book end with the death and burial of Moses.

Review

✠ What books of the Bible are included in the Torah?

✠ What history does the Book of Genesis cover?

✠ What history does the Book of Exodus cover?

✠ What are the central concerns of the Books of Leviticus, Numbers, and Deuteronomy?

Reflection

✠ God selected the family of Abraham as God's Chosen People. How well are you living your faith as a member of God's chosen Christian people?

✠ The law God gave to the Hebrew nation was sacred. How sacred are the laws of God to us?

II. THE FORMER PROPHETS

After the death of Moses, God gave the Israelites a new leader named Joshua. "Now Joshua, son of Nun, was filled with the spirit of wisdom, since Moses had laid his hands upon him; and so the Israelites gave him their obedience, just as the LORD had commanded Moses" (Deuteronomy 34:9).

In the Torah, "prophet" refers to someone who functions as a vehicle of communication between God and human beings and vice versa. The Hebrew Bible lists the books of Joshua, Judges, 1 and 2 Samuel, and 1 and 2 Kings under the heading of the Books of the Prophets, while current translations position them under historical narratives. God not only led the people through the desert to the Promised Land, but God continued to be with the people as they became a people of the land instead of wanderers in the desert. The prophets in these books, known as the Former Prophets, were legitimate prophets speaking for God, and the books themselves speak of God's dealings with his Chosen People. The prophets communicated with God through visions, dreams, and divinations.

Another group of prophets that appeared during the time of the monarchy and were known as the Latter Prophets. They anointed and challenged kings, warning them through prophecies about some disaster awaiting them if the kings did not repent of some sinful actions. The Latter Prophets' writings are found in the Bible.

The books of the Former Prophets describe a period that includes: (1) Joshua's conquest of the land of Canaan (in the Book of Joshua), (2) the emergence of the "people of Israel" as independent states during the "premonarchic" period of the judges (in the Book of Judges), (3) and the period when kings replaced judges as rulers in the monarchic period (in the books of 1 and 2 Samuel and 1 and 2 Kings), with the anointing of Saul in 1 Samuel.

The third period of the Former Prophets can be further divided into three periods. The first included the united monarchy during the time of Kings Saul and David (1 and 2 Samuel) and the reign of King Solomon (1

Kings). The second period included the story of the divided monarchy in 1 Kings, when the kingdoms were divided into the northern kingdom of Israel and the southern kingdom of Judah (1 Kings). It accounted for the fall of the capital of the northern kingdom, Samaria, under the siege of the Assyrian army. In the third period, the kingdom of Judah fell under the onslaught of the Babylonian invasion (2 Kings).

The Book of Joshua

After the death of Moses, Joshua led the Hebrew people into the Promised Land and guided them in capturing it. The land God promised to the Israelites did not fall into their hands easily. They had to fight many battles with the inhabitants in order to conquer the land, and there still remained more to be conquered when Joshua died.

Fall of Jericho

God directed Joshua through a vision about the miraculous capture of Jericho, where the walls came tumbling down when the Israelites let out a colossal noise. Throughout his rule, Joshua received messages from God and conveyed them to the people. Joshua died and was buried in the Promised Land, as were the bones of Joseph, which the Israelites had carried from Egypt.

Division of the Land

When areas of the Promised Land were conquered, each of the tribes of Israel (Jacob's sons) received a portion of the land for its possession, with the exception of the tribe of Levi. Members of the tribe of Levi were chosen to serve as priests for all the tribes. Joseph's two sons received two portions, and the land was divided into twelve sections. The ten tribes that settled to the north of Jerusalem were often in conflict with the two tribes that settled to the south of Jerusalem. Besides fighting outside forces, the tribes from the north and the south found themselves in clashes with each other.

The Book of Judges

When the Hebrew people first settled in the Promised Land, they lived under the leadership and protection of twelve courageous men and women who were known as judges. They were not the kind of judges we have today, but they were leaders sent by God. The Book of Judges details lengthy stories of six of the judges who comprised a group known as the major judges. Six other judges that the book presents in summary fashion were known as the minor judges. Eli the high priest and Samuel the prophet were two judges not found in the Book of Judges but in the book that follows, 1 Samuel. The two of them seem to have ruled Israel until the institution of the monarchy. When the Israelites disobeyed the covenant, pagan nations successfully oppressed them. When they repented and remained loyal, God raised up heroic judges to lead them:

—***Deborah and Barak:*** They gathered an army of 10,000 men to fight the Canaanites.

—***Gideon:*** With a force of only 300 men, Gideon defeated the Midianites. His son, Abimelech, ruled for a short time but was eventually killed.

—***Samson:*** Known for his betrayal by Delilah, Samson led no army but with great strength fought against the Philistines. He eventually killed 3,000 Philistines in their temple.

—***Jephthah:*** Before defeating the Ammonites, Jephthah foolishly vowed to God that he would sacrifice the first person to greet him after the battle if God helped bring about a victory. He won the battle, his daughter greeted him first, and he fulfilled his vow.

The First Book of Samuel

The First Book of Samuel includes the period from the birth of Samuel the prophet to the death of King Saul and his sons. It is the period when Israel inaugurates its choice of a king for Israel and when the sins of the first king take place.

The Birth of Samuel

The book begins with Hanna, the mother of Samuel, whose prayer for a child is answered after a long period of praying. She dedicates the child to the service of the Lord under the priest Eli, leaving him in the temple with the priest. Samuel grew to become known as an accredited prophet. In 1 Samuel, we read: "Thus all Israel from Dan to Beer-sheba came to know that Samuel was an accredited prophet of the LORD" (1 Samuel 3:20). When Samuel grew old, he appointed his two sons as judges of the people, but his sons were corrupt, and the people sought to be led by a king instead of judges.

Saul, the First King of Israel

God was the *true* king of the people of Israel, but the people wanted the type of kingdom found among the powerful nations that surrounded them. When they began to clamor for a king, God resisted their call at first, but God finally relented and sent Samuel to anoint Saul as the first king of Israel. Saul began his rule with great piety but ended it in idolatry and jealousy. The Philistines eventually slaughtered Saul and his sons. The First Book of Samuel ends with the burial of Saul.

The Second Book of Samuel

Second Samuel covers the period from the choosing of David as Israel's king to the need for an offering made by David to rid the land of a pestilence. God cast a pestilence on the land because David sinned by calling for a census.

David Captures Jerusalem

Israel's second king, David, who was also anointed as king by Samuel, became the great king in Israelite history. He was not the most powerful of the Israelite kings, but he was the most revered and the one who brought the northern and southern tribes together.

David wisely captured the city of Jerusalem, which was outside the boundaries of all the tribes, and made it the holy city for all of Israel by bringing the Ark of the Covenant to Jerusalem. The Scriptures portray David as a great lover of God, a man who committed grave and thoughtless sins but who always repented. David had a great regard for the covenant. The people, through the later preaching of the prophets, came to believe that the "one to come," the Messiah, would come from the line of David. Samuel, Nathan, and Gad are prophets found in the story of David.

The Land

It is difficult for us to understand what "the land" meant to the people of Israel. Around the time of David, the people began to see the land as a gift that God promised them. It was the Promised Land. The land, for the Israelite, was sacred. Although the Scriptures speak of the Promised Land earlier in history, many commentators believe that it was only during the reign of David that this idea really began to develop. The people of David's time presumed that the people of the past felt the same love and yearning for the Promised Land as they did.

Because land was a gift from God, the people of Israel believed they had a duty to keep the land out of the hands of foreign invaders. They also believed God would help them in this endeavor. The land became the Holy Land, the place where God dwelt with the people. Many believe that possession of the land was necessary for the preservation of the true faith of the Israelite nation.

The Book of Ruth

The Book of Ruth does not belong to the series of books known as the Former Prophets, but the story of Ruth, David's grandmother, fittingly belongs in the history segment of the Bible since her story precedes that of David's. Ruth is a Moabite woman, not a Jew, who marries Boaz, David's grandfather. Her marriage into the family line of David becomes a story for Jews as well as gentiles (non-Jews), since she is a gentile. It also connects her to the family line of Jesus. The story presents Ruth as a pious, faith-filled, dedicated, and loving daughter-in-law of Naomi. The book is famous for the lines Ruth spoke to Naomi (1:16): "Wherever you go I will

two tribes

go, wherever you lodge I will lodge. Your people shall be my people and your God, my God."

The First Book of Kings

The First Book of Kings begins with David as an old man who must choose a successor.

Solomon Becomes King

Before David died, he passed on his reign to his son, Solomon, who became the most powerful king in Israelite history. Because David was more of a warrior-type leader with "blood on his hands," God would not allow him to build the Temple. The task of building this magnificent structure would belong to Solomon.

The Temple in Judaism

The majestic Temple that Solomon built became the center of Jewish worship. The holy city of Jerusalem was central to Jewish life, and central to this great city was the Temple. On important feasts, Jews from all over came to the Temple to worship. Central to the Temple was the altar of sacrifice, where priests offered sacrifices in the name of the people. Each day, sacrifices were offered in the Temple, and on great feasts many more sacrifices were offered. The holy city, the Temple, the altar of sacrifice, and the priesthood were central to Judaism, even in the time of Jesus.

A Kingdom Divided

When Solomon died, Rehoboam, a son of Solomon, was accepted as king by the two tribes to the south (Benjamin and Judah). Before the ten tribes of the north would accept Rehoboam, however, they requested leniency on taxes and other laws. Rehoboam, following the advice of younger consultants, refused to grant this leniency and, as a result, was rejected by the northern tribes who, in 922 BC, chose a man named Jeroboam to lead them. This split the Israelite nation into two weak factions—the ten tribes to the north (Israel) and the two tribes to the south (Judah).

North: Isreal led by Rehoboam son of Solomon
South: Judah led by Jeroboam

Prophets for the Kingdoms

Throughout the history of both the northern and southern kingdoms, God continued to show concern for both factions. Prophets were sent to the kings who followed the reign of Jeroboam in the north, the kingdom of Israel, and to the kings who followed Rehoboam in the south, the kingdom of Judah. They warned the kings of the need to remain faithful to the law and the one true God, but many of the kings refused to listen to the prophets. The prophets saw this refusal as a cause for the downfall of both kingdoms. God chose Elijah and Elisha to prophesy in the northern kingdom (Israel).

The Second Book of Kings

The Second Book of Kings begins with confrontations between Elijah and the kings and Elisha, the successor of Elijah, and ends with the Babylonian conquest of Judah.

The Assyrian Invasion of Israel

In 721 BC, the Assyrian army invaded the northern kingdom, captured the land, and destroyed the monarchy in the north. It led some of the inhabitants into exile and brought exiles from other countries into the area to mix and intermarry with those who remained. This mixing of people from different countries was a military tactic that left conquered countries with a lack of unity. Since the people mistrusted exiles from other countries, they could not unite to form any type of rebellion against the conquering country.

In time, the people of the north began to intermarry with exiles from other countries and thus lost their pure Israelite identity. The former inhabitants of the area of the kingdom of Israel came to be known as Samaritans. With the intermarriage that took place and the total annihilation of the northern kingdom, the animosity between Samaria and Judah grew into a strong prejudice that still existed during the life of Jesus.

Babylonian Captivity

In 587 BC, it was Judah's turn to face destruction. The powerful nation of Babylon invaded Jerusalem and its surrounding area, slaughtered many of its inhabitants, and led the remaining survivors on a death march to Babylon. A state of confusion filled the hearts of many of the Israelites. The sacred land, the foundation of their nation and their religion, had been lost. Those with a strong faith were able to keep alive the hope that God would, somehow, against overwhelming odds, keep the promises made to the people of Israel in the past. The devastation and cruelty of the incident burned itself into the minds of the Jewish nation for centuries to come. Jesus would have learned about the invasion, the slaughter, and the exile endured by the Israelites in slavery in Babylon.

The Diaspora

Some of the inhabitants of Judea who foresaw the impending invasion fled into Egypt and other areas north of Palestine to escape it. The Jewish communities that sprang up outside Palestine as a result of this flight from the Promised Land eventually came to be known as the Diaspora, which means "the dispersion." These people still considered Palestine their homeland and, in later centuries after Jerusalem and the Temple were rebuilt, they would return in pilgrimage for the major Jewish feasts.

Review

- ✠ Who were the Former Prophets?
- ✠ Why was God displeased when the Israelites asked for a king?
- ✠ What led to the division of the kingdom of Israel?
- ✠ What was the Diaspora?

Reflection

- ✠ Moses passed on his power to Joshua by laying hands on him. In baptism, the presider laid hands on you as a gesture of passing on a sacramental gift given to the Church by Christ. How well are you fulfilling your call to reflect the presence of Christ in the world?
- ✠ Saul was a faithful Israelite when he was made king, but he turned away from God and lost God's favor. What warning can we take from the story of Saul?
- ✠ The Babylonian captivity was a dreadful memory for generations long after it occurred. Why does God allow such horrors as the Babylonian captivity and the Holocaust to happen?

CHAPTER THREE

History After the Exile

I. THE CHRONICLER'S HISTORY

About fifty years after the Babylonian captivity, in 538 BC, the people in exile in Babylon had to face a new decision. Many had grown up in Babylon and had learned to call it home. When the Persians overran the Babylonian Empire in 538 BC, they permitted the Judeans to return home. Many chose to stay in Babylon, while a remnant chose to return to the Promised Land of their ancestors. The Hebrews originally settled in the Promised Land with the twelve tribes of Israel, but after the Assyrian and Babylonian invasions, only one tribe remained: the tribe of Judah. The Israelites became identified under the name of the one tribe of Judah and became known to many as Jews.

An enthusiastic group returned home to Judea and began to rebuild the Temple and the holy city. The Temple and city were rebuilt by 516 BC, and the walls of the city were completed by 450 BC. Although they now lived under Persian rule, the people of Judea lived their religious faith in virtual freedom.

First and Second Chronicles

The Books of Chronicles duplicate the story of the Hebrew nation from Saul to the exile, filling the extensive period with genealogies and other details. It must be read as "sacred history," which does not have as its purpose to present accurate history in our modern sense but stresses that God is at work in history.

The Books of Ezra and Nehemiah

The Books of Ezra and Nehemiah explain the arrival in Jerusalem and the restoration of the altar and the Temple. In a pivotal point in the Book of Nehemia, Ezra opens the scroll of the Law and reads and interprets it for the people, who were standing and weeping. Ezra tells the people that it is a time for rejoicing, not for weeping. The dedication of a wall built around Jerusalem was also an occasion for joy. The Chronicler wrote his books around 400 BC.

The Books of Tobit, Judith, and Esther

The Books of Tobit, Judith, and Esther do not belong to the Chronicler's history, but they are present among the history books. They present fascinating stories of people of faith who have great trust in God. The authors of the books are indifferent to historical accuracy. These three books, along with the Books of 1 and 2 Maccabees, come under the category of Biblical Novellas, which means they are edifying stories. The Books of Maccabees have a closer link with historical accuracy, but they present a heroic and embellished image of Jewish leaders who rebel against the intrusion of Greek culture and religious practice in Israel. The author speaks of the warrior, Judas Maccabeus, in glowing terms: "In his deeds he was like a lion, like a young lion roaring for prey" (1 Maccabees 3:4).

The Book of Tobit presents the story of a virtuous man who shares his spiritual wisdom through his actions and words. He writes of his virtue in his book: "I, Tobit, have walked all the days of my life on paths of fidelity and righteousness" (Tobit 1:3).

The Book of Judith includes a story about the victory of the Chosen People over the enemy through the intervention of a woman. Judith lures a general named Holofernes, an enemy of Israel, to accept her into his bedroom and beheads him as he slept. The people see her as a champion for her deed. They declare, "You are the glory of Jerusalem! You are the great pride of Israel! You are the great boast of our nation" (Judith 15:9)!

The Book of Esther also tells a story of victory accomplished through the actions of a woman who turns those who were to massacre the Jews into being massacred themselves. Most Protestant Bibles place the books of Tobit and Judith under the heading of "apocrypha," while the Catholic Church places them under the heading of "deuterocanonical."

First and Second Maccabees

The Books of Maccabees were written about a hundred years before Christ. The Second Book of Maccabees does not continue where the first book ends but offers a modified account of events related in the first seven chapters of the previous book. The books are better understood in the historical context of the era.

The Influence of Alexander the Great

Throughout history, certain people have influence that reaches far beyond their own time. Such a person was Alexander the Great, who became the ruler of Macedon in 334 BC, and by 332 BC he set out to conquer the Persian Empire. He pushed his forces as far east as India and as far south as Egypt, making the Greek Empire the greatest power of the day. The people of Judea, as well as many others in the world, welcomed the great conquests with hope that a new age of freedom would dawn. At the age of thirty-three, in 323 BC, Alexander the Great died, and his empire was split among warring generals.

Alexander brought to his empire a love for Greek culture, and he spread this culture throughout the empire with the zeal of a missionary. He was a student of the philosopher Aristotle and had studied Greek culture and arts during his younger days. He sought to have the whole world speaking Greek and living according to Greek ways. Even after this death, Greek culture continued to flourish.

Hellenization

Alexander did not wish to destroy the basic cultures of his empire. He did, however, want them to be mixed with Greek culture in such a way that Greek influence might enrich them and be even more dominant. As mentioned earlier, this process of mixing Greek culture with other cultures was called Hellenization.

The Jewish people profited and suffered from this imposition of Greek culture. The use of the common Greek language throughout the world enabled Jews to translate the Hebrew Bible into Greek for those Jews of the Diaspora who did not speak Hebrew. Because Jews allowed no outside influence in their own country and traditions, they resisted the Greek influence within Judea and established themselves as enemies of Hellenization. This caused great suffering for the people of Judea.

Antiochus IV

After Alexander's death, two of his generals fought for control of the areas around Judea. The Jews soon found themselves sandwiched between two of these factions, captive first to one and then to the other great power. Despite this foreign domination, Jews lived in comparative freedom until 175 BC. In that year, a ruler named Antiochus IV ruled the Seleucid dynasty, which included the land of Judea and a large portion of the countries north and east of Judea. Antiochus sought to Hellenize all of his possessions as well as to levy heavy taxes upon these possessions to pay for his war efforts. The heavy taxes and forced Hellenization caused a growing discontent among the Jewish people.

In 168 BC, Antiochus IV issued an edict that ordered death to those who celebrated religious feasts, honored the Sabbath, or allowed circumcision. He further ordered that all manuscripts of the Torah be destroyed. Pagan altars began to appear throughout Judea, and Jews were ordered to worship pagan gods. The greatest insult to Judaism came when the statue of the Greek god Zeus was placed in the Jewish Temple. To ensure that his edict would be enforced, Antiochus sent his troops to police the land.

After the return of the Jews from Babylon centuries earlier, their religious leader was the high priest. Since religious life and daily life were so closely linked, this made the high priest a person of great influence in the lives of the Jewish people. Antiochus realized the political advantage of having a high priest who supported him, so he appointed his own high priest. He chose a man who would pay well for the office, collect high taxes from the people, and support Hellenization.

Mattathias Leads a Revolt

The Jewish revolt began innocently enough, at least in the eyes of Antiochus. A man named Mattathias refused to offer a sacrifice to a false god and killed a Jew about to offer a sacrifice. He likewise killed a guard who brought the order to the village in which Mattathias lived. As a result, Mattathias, his five sons, and some followers fled to the hills. The event might have seemed insignificant to Antiochus, but the family would eventually become well-known in Jewish history as the Hasmoneans. After the death of Mattathias, his son, Judas, hammered away at the enemy with guerilla tactics until a general of Antiochus' army agreed to a peace treaty. Judas received the nickname Maccabeus, meaning "hammer," which gave the revolt its name, the Maccabean Revolt.

A great celebration took place in 165 BC, when Judas cleansed and rededicated the Temple. Even today, Jews recall this event with the feast of Hanukkah, which is also called the Festival of Lights. With religious freedom, some of the Jewish people wanted to continue to press for political freedom. They felt it was not right for the Holy Land to be held under foreign domination. Under the leadership of Simon, a brother of Judas, some status of independence was gained as the last strongholds of the foreign rulers were overcome. Although Simon did not belong to the priestly family, he was made the legitimate high priest until a suitable representative could be found. This, in effect, made him the ruler of the people.

The Ark of the Covenant

The Ark of the Covenant was a sacred golden chest described in the Book of Exodus as containing the tablets of stone on which the Ten Commandments were inscribed. It held a place of high respect in the life of the Israelite people. According to the Book of Exodus, God commanded Moses on Mount Sinai to build the ark and gave instructions for its construction.

The ark was completely covered with gold, with two rings of gold on each side and poles overlaid with gold passing through these rings for carrying the ark. Two golden cherubim (angels) were mounted on top of the ark, with a footstool in the middle where the feet of the invisible God rested. According to the commandments, the Israelites were not permitted to make any image of God. The Levites were appointed to minister before the ark.

The biblical account relates that during the Israelites' exodus from Egypt, the priests carried the ark a short distance in front of the people. Whenever the Israelites camped, the ark was placed in a special, sacred tent called a tabernacle. At the end of the exodus, when the priests bearing the ark stepped into the bed of the Jordan, the water in the river separated, opening a path for the Israelites to pass through to Jericho. As long as the priests remained in the bed of the river with the ark, the people were able to pass through. At Jericho, the Israelites marched around the walls of the city, following the ark for seven days. On the seventh day, the walls tumbled when the people shouted and seven priests who were marching in front of the ark blew their horns. Jericho was destroyed.

After the Israelites settled in the Promised Land, they had to fight against the Philistines. The ark that was carried in battle was captured twice by the Philistines but returned after an affliction of tumors, boils, and rats plagued the Philistine population.

At the beginning of his reign, King David decided to bring the ark to Zion. On the journey, one of the drivers of the cart carrying the ark put out his hand to steady the ark, which was tipping off the cart, and God killed him for touching the ark. David, frightened by the incident, brought the ark to the house of a man named Obededom the Gittite instead of having it carried to Zion, and there it remained for three months. Later, hearing that God had blessed Obededom because of the presence of the ark in his house, David ordered the ark brought to Zion by the Levites, while he himself, girded with a linen apron, danced before the Lord with all his might in view of the crowds in Jerusalem. When Saul's daughter, Michal, saw this, she rebuked him. In Zion, David put the ark in the tabernacle he had prepared for it, offered sacrifices, celebrating by distributing food and blessing the people.

David's plan of building a temple for the ark ceased at the advice of God, who spoke to David through the prophet Nathan. Finally, during the construction of Solomon's Temple, a special inner room, named the Holy of Holies, was prepared to house the ark. When the priests emerged from the holy place after placing the ark there, the temple was filled with a cloud, "for the glory of the Lord had filled the house of the Lord." In 586 BC, the Babylonians destroyed Jerusalem and Solomon's Temple. There is no record of what became of the ark.

The Synagogue

Although the Jewish people living outside Jerusalem longed to return to the holy city for the great Jewish feasts, they were not always able to do so. The true center of Jewish worship was the Temple, and the one Temple of Judaism was situated in Jerusalem. Since many of the people fled from Palestine around the time of the Babylonian invasion in 586 BC, it seems logical that this is the period when the need for synagogues began. The people quite naturally developed a way to keep alive their community worship of God without the Temple. This new type of worship happened in a synagogue, with worship taking place on the Sabbath and on certain festivals. The synagogue became the center of Jewish life, used for Scripture studies and places for educating children and adults. It did not have the deep ceremonial worship found in the Temple, nor did sacrifices happen there.

When a learned rabbi, such as Jesus, would come into the synagogue for the first time, the people would invite him to lead the study and interpretation of the Scriptures. The synagogue became an important fixture within Judaism not only for those who lived a great distance from the Temple, but also during those periods when the Temple was destroyed and not yet rebuilt. In this way, the unity of religion and daily life was kept alive for the Jewish communities. Luke reports in his Gospel that Jesus went into the synagogue on the Sabbath, "as was his custom."

The Wisdom Books

The Wisdom Books in the Bible have their roots in ancient Near East wisdom literature, a type of writing that centers on life's questions about God, creation, and the nature of evil and suffering in the world. The Israelite people believed in the one true God, and they adapted much of ancient Near East wisdom literature with God in mind. The aim was not only to address how to live in the world but how to live in God's world. Through wise sayings, poetry, prayers, dialogue, or love songs, the various Wisdom writers in the Bible developed a successful response to living in a world created by God. The books make use of parallelism, which is identified by balanced phrases typical of Hebrew poetry. The Wisdom Books are Job, Psalms, Proverbs, Ecclesiastes, Song of Songs, Wisdom, and Sirach (Ecclesiasticus).

—*The Book of Job:* The Book of Job presents the story of a just man who faces the problems and questions of suffering while remaining faithful to God. Job faces his first great loss of animals, sons, and daughters by proclaiming, "Naked I came forth from my mother's womb, and naked shall I go back there. The LORD gave and the LORD has taken away; blessed be the name of the LORD" (Job 1:21)!

—*The Book of Psalms:* The Book of Psalms consists of a compilation of prayers, hymns, and poems that convey the religious experience of Jews throughout their history. They speak of joy, hope, frustration, questioning, but most often end with trust in God. There are 150 psalms.

—*The Book of Proverbs:* The title of the Book of Proverbs describes the book almost to perfection. It is a book dedicated to teaching wisdom to the young. In Proverbs, we read, "Be not wise in your own eyes, fear the LORD and turn away from evil" (Proverbs 3:7).

—*The Book of Ecclesiastes:* Although the book recognizes there is a divine plan hidden from humans, it is a skeptical book, noting that all is vanity and empty in this world. It has no intention of leading the reader to gloom or hopelessness. Although all is vanity, the book calls upon the reader to thank God for the pleasures one finds in life. The author writes: "Remember your Creator in the days of your youth, before the evil days come" (Ecclesiastes 12:1).

—*Song of Songs:* Song of Songs is a poetic form of literature that presents the Lord as a lover and human beings as the beloved. In some intimate detail, it presents an ideal image of love that exists between God and human beings. The author begins his text with the words, "Let him kiss me with kisses of his mouth, for your love is better than wine" (Song of Songs 1:2).

—*The Book of Wisdom:* The Book of Wisdom, written about a hundred years before Christ, uses popular religious themes to edify its readers at a time when they are enduring torment and oppression. The author writes of trust in God: "Love righteousness, you who judge the earth; think of the LORD in goodness, and seek him in integrity of heart" (Wisdom 1:1).

—*The Book of Sirach (Ecclesiasticus):* The Book of Sirach includes sayings that seek to motivate readers to maintain their religious faith and fidelity to God and one another through an understanding of the sacred manuscripts and tradition. We read, "Do not delay turning back to the LORD, do not put it off day after day" (Sirach 5:7).

Review

✠ What books of the Bible referred to the settling of the Israelites back in the Promised Land after the exile?

✠ What was the influence of Alexander the Great on the history of Israel?

✠ Why was the Ark of the Covenant important?

✠ What was the origin of the synagogue?

Reflection

✠ When the people returned to the Promised Land from exile, they wept as Ezra the priest read the Law to them. How do you feel about the sacredness of the law of love and forgiveness given to us by Christ?

✠ The Book of Maccabees describes a type of holy war against paganism. Does the story have a message for those seeking to understand the meaning of a just war as opposed to those who believe we should never have wars?

✠ The Ark of the Covenant held a sacred and central spot in Israelite history. Are there similarities and dissimilarities between the reverence for the ark and the honor given to the Eucharist in the Roman Catholic Church or in Eastern Christianity?

II. GOD SPEAKS THROUGH THE PROPHETS

God chose the prophets as reported in Jeremiah: "The word of the LORD came to me: Before I formed you in the womb I knew you, before you were born I dedicated you, a prophet to the nations I appointed you" (Jeremiah 1:4–5). Prophets wrote before, during, and after the exile.

The Prophetic Books

The word of God comes to us in various literary forms in the Bible. In this section, the inspired word of God speaks to us in the language of prophecy and with the highly symbolic language of apocalyptic writings. Through it all, the believer learns how to relate to a loving God. God challenges the people, warns them, and encourages them in the midst of persecution and death. The God of love is always present, standing at the center of Israelite history.

In a scriptural sense, a prophet was one who spoke or acted in the name of God. Since they often had to remind the nation of the sins it was committing against the one true God and the dire consequences of these sins for the nation, prophets were often not popular with the people and kings. Some would warn of future catastrophes that the nation would endure, such as the annihilation of the northern kingdom of Israel by the Assyrians, the Babylonian invasion of Judea, and the exile in Babylon. Prophets also predicted a day when the Israelites would be freed from their exile and allowed to return home.

The Prophetic Books include the names of four major and twelve minor prophets, along with the Books of Lamentations and Baruch. The designations of major and minor refer to the length of the manuscripts, not that one is more important than the other.

The four major prophets are: Isaiah, Jeremiah, Ezekiel, and Daniel.

The twelve minor prophets are: Hosea, Joel, Amos, Obadiah, Jonah, Micah, Nahum, Habakkuk, Haggai, Zephaniah, Zechariah, and Malachi.

The Book of Isaiah

Most commentators recognize that the Book of Isaiah is not the work of a single author but of a number of writers. Three breaks are found in the book, leading commentators to surmise there were three different writers. The "first" Book of Isaiah (chapters 1–39) deals with Yahweh's special relationship with the Davidic kings in Jerusalem and Isaiah's warnings against establishing an alliance with the Assyrians. The "second" (chapters 40–55) is attributed to an unknown author whose works are in Isaiah and who prophesied during the end of the Babylonian exile. The "third" (chapters 56–66) collects later oracles written or preached by disciples of Isaiah. Also within Isaiah are passages other authors wrote.

The Book of Jeremiah

The Book of Jeremiah is the work of a prophet who prophesied in the southern kingdom from the last quarter of the seventh century BC to the early part of the sixth century BC. It combines history, biography, oracles, prayers, poems, and exhortations. Jeremiah confronts the idolatry in Judah and faces persecution for his endeavors. He foresees the disaster to be endured by the nation at the hands of Babylonians.

The Book of Lamentations

The Book of Lamentations contains five laments over the destruction of Jerusalem written by an author who witnessed the destruction of Jerusalem in 587 BC. The Lamentations speak of the flaws of humans and the strength and love of God. The laments were dirges chanted in mourning by Jews each year in memory of the destruction of the holy city.

The Book of Baruch

Although the Book of Baruch is attributed to a well-known secretary and companion of Jeremiah, it is most likely a compilation of works written by at least three different authors. The book includes five diverse compositions, with the first and the fifth in prose and the middle three in poetry. It ranges from the pious reflections on the circumstances of the exiles in Babylonian captivity to a supposed letter of Jeremiah against idolatry.

The Book of Ezekiel

Ezekiel prophesized during the early Babylonian exile in 597 BC and was the first prophet to prophecy outside of Israel. He wrote of the total destruction of Jerusalem that was yet to take place and eventually offers hope. Ezekiel shows a great interest in the Temple and the liturgy, and speaks of a new covenant along with the conditions necessary to attain it. The book exhibits clear signs of editing and text added later by postexilic survivors.

The Book of Daniel

The Book of Daniel, composed during the persecution by Antiochus IV near the middle of the second century BC, is the story of a young Jew who lived in exile in Babylon in the eighth century BC. The book actually belongs to the apocalyptic writings. It contains an apocalyptic presentation aimed at providing encouragement to Jews in the midst of persecution, reminding them that despite the torment they endure, God is still in control.

The Book of Hosea

The Book of Hosea addresses the infidelity of the northern kingdom during the middle of the eighth century BC. Hosea tells the story of an unfaithful wife, Gomer, who represents Israel, and the faithful husband who experiences the grief endured by his situation. The faithful husband is like Yahweh, who punishes but never abandons Israel.

The Book of Joel

The Book of Joel includes apocalyptic imagery. The book, written around the fifth century BC, describes an invasion of locusts that was taking place in Judah as a sign of the coming day of the Lord. The prophet calls for an assembly of the people where they are to repent and have the priests pray for the people. As a result of the prayerful assembly, the Lord promises to end the locust assault and bestow blessings on the land.

The Book of Amos

Amos prophesied in the northern kingdom during the reign of Jeroboam II, who brings some stability to the northern kingdom. Amos challenges the idolatry and injustice found in Israel and threatens that the day of Yahweh would be a day of darkness when the Assyrian invasion would conquer the northern kingdom of Israel and its inhabitants. His unwelcome message causes him a great deal of torment and ridicule.

The Book of Obadiah

The Book of Obadiah, most likely written in the fifth century BC, chastises Edom, a perpetual enemy of Israel. When the Israelites return from the exile, they must fight to regain portions of the land, and Edom is one of the enemies they encounter. In this shortest book of prophecy, the prophet speaks of Edom being ravaged and Judah and Israel being again united as one.

The Book of Jonah

The Book of Jonah, written after the exile in the fifth century BC, presents the picture of a reluctant prophet whom God miraculously brings to the shores of Nineveh to convert the inhabitants. To the unhappiness of Jonah, the people of the hated Assyrian city of Nineveh repent in sackcloth and ashes. The story's theme reminds the Hebrews that a people as wicked as those of Nineveh could repent and avert God's wrath.

The Book of Micah

Micah, a contemporary of Isaiah, attacks the unjust wealthy, cheating merchants, and the dishonest priests and prophets in Samaria and Jerusalem. Although he speaks of reproaches and warnings of punishment, Micah concludes each time with a message of hope and promise.

The Book of Nahum

In the Book of Nahum, the prophet rejoices over the impending doom of the despised city of Nineveh in Assyria that takes place in 612 BC. The cause of his joy comes from an awareness of the bitter atrocities inflicted upon the people by the Assyrians, but he also tempers his joy by recognizing that God is not a God of vengeance but a God of mercy.

The Book of Habakkuk

Habakkuk writes toward the end of the seventh century BC and the beginning of the sixth century BC at a time when the Babylonians are threatening to destroy Judah. According to Habakkuk, God has prepared a chastisement for Judah at the hands of the Babylonians. Because of the corruption of Judah, God will be an avenging rod, but the faithful will survive.

The Book of Haggai

Haggai is a postexilic prophet (520 BC) who exhorts and encourages the population to build the second Temple. He speaks of the future magnificence of the new Temple exceeding that of the previous one.

The Book of Zephaniah

Zephaniah writes during the reign of King Josiah (640–609 BC), before a reform Josiah initiated. The people are deeply affected by Assyrian influence, which involves Judah's worship of foreign gods and which the people's leaders refuse to challenge. Zephaniah speaks of the destruction and death that God will bring upon Judah and Jerusalem. He foresees a universal wreckage in which every form of life will be annihilated. He states that the day of the Lord will be one of unimaginable devastation.

The Book of Zechariah

The Book of Zechariah dates to 520 BC. The first eight chapters belong to the original author. They contain eight visions relating to the building of the Temple and offer encouragement to those who returned from exile. The last six chapters contain the work of one or more anonymous writers, including oracles about the coming Prince of Peace and an apocalyptic image of the final assault of the enemy on Jerusalem, after which the messianic era will begin.

The Book of Malachi

The Book of Malachi, written by an unknown author around the middle of the fifth century BC, demonstrates Yahweh's displeasure with the people for a multitude of offenses that include using inferior animals for sacrifice, failing in matters of tithes and offerings, and men divorcing their wives to marry women of foreign ancestry. The book concludes that the day of the Lord is coming, but first God will send someone to prepare the way for the Lord. Then the day of judgment will arrive.

Apocalyptic Literature

Apocalyptic literature consists of a form of writing found in some books of the Bible and other works. It has its origin in a Greek word that means "something revealed," and its origins lie in the third and second centuries before the Jesus' birth. Long after the people settled in Israel and the period of prophecy ended, a new form of spiritual literature emerged known as apocalyptic literature. Apocalyptic literature concerned itself with "the last things."

Two Ages—Evil and Glorious

Apocalyptic literature separates time and history into two categories: the present evil age and a glorious new age. It speaks of the end of the present evil age and the beginning of the new age. The writings portray how the world will reach this glorious new age, usually by describing a cosmic conflict between God and Satan and their powerful armies. It is both pessimistic when viewing the impossibility of human beings in bringing about a solution to their present oppressive condition and optimistic when viewing the power of God, who is always in control and who will triumph. Apocalyptic writings were intended for the immediate future, not for people living hundreds or thousands of years in the future. The signs and warnings found in apocalyptic writings were not meant to deliver hints about the imminence of the end of the world.

Apocalypse of Daniel

The best-known of the early Jewish apocalypses takes place in the final part of the Book of Daniel (chapters 7–12), which speaks of beasts, angels, and wars. The book, as mentioned above in the prophets section, is attributed to a revered wise man who lived some four centuries earlier at the time of the Babylonian captivity. Some commentators do not list Daniel among the major prophets, but they identify him as an apocalyptic writer. These chapters in the Book of Daniel speak symbolically of a conflict that overwhelms the beast, who is apparently Antiochus IV.

New Testament Apocalypse

The New Testament closes with the most famous apocalyptic book known to most Christians, the Book of Revelation. The author, who pretends to be living in the past and predicting future events and persecutions when he is actually living while the events are taking place, used apocalyptic literature as a code for Christians being persecuted by the Romans. Through the symbolism found in apocalyptic writing, Christians are encouraged to endure their persecution, knowing that some day God will triumph over the beast, and the saints will enjoy a new and glorious day with the Lord. The New Testament includes other apocalyptic writings found in short passages of the Gospels and in some letters written by the early disciples of Jesus. Apocalyptic writings such as the books of Daniel and Revelation emerged at times of crisis to encourage the faithful.

Characteristics of Apocalyptic Literature

Apocalyptic writings differ from prophetic writings in several ways. The author is usually depicted as some well-known figure who lived before the actual events took place, thus enabling the unknown author to present current history as though he were predicting it from a past viewpoint. The writings make use of highly symbolic language, including beasts, idols, dragons, or other monstrous animals when referring to pagan kings or nations. There are usually an abundance of angels in apocalyptic writings. The writings predict unbearable calamities such as plagues, disease, wars, earthquakes, or other afflictions as signs that the end of the world is near. The writings often depict God as an enthroned king. A significant aspect of apocalyptic writings is that they speak of everlasting life, a new development in religious thinking beginning for the most part in the second century BC and continuing to our present era.

Review

✠ What do commentators believe about the authors of the Book of Isaiah?

✠ What is a common message found in many of the writings of the prophets?

✠ What is apocalyptic literature?

Reflection

✠ God sent prophets at times of conflict or danger. Do you believe the world has prophets sent by God today?

✠ Some believe apocalyptic writings tell us when the world will end. What is the value of apocalyptic literature today?

CHAPTER FOUR

Life in Palestine in Jesus' Day

I. THE POLITICAL AND RELIGIOUS ENVIRONMENT OF JESUS' DAY

As often happens with revolts motivated by high ideals, the aims of future leaders did not always match the noble ones of earlier commanders. The situation began to deteriorate after the period of the Maccabees. Among the leaders who followed Simon was his son, Alexander Jannaeus, who came to power in 103 BC. Alexander sought to restore the ancient boundaries of the Davidic kingdom into the hands of Judaism, thus making it a more powerful nation. Unfortunately, his endeavors led him into conflict with the people of Judaism, as well as with those outside Judaism. Many believed that Alexander Jannaeus had abandoned the ideals of the Maccabean Revolt.

After the death of Alexander Jannaeus, the breakdown of the independent Jewish kingdom was not far off. Alexander's wife, Alexandra, ruled for ten years after his death, and she was able to bring some stability to the Jewish nation. At her death in 67 BC, the nation broke into fragments over her successor. Some wanted the first of her sons to rule, others wanted a second son to rule, and still others wanted neither of them. All three factions sent delegations to Pompey, a Roman general who was in Syria at the time. Pompey, taking advantage of the lack of unity among the Jewish people, responded with an invasion of the land, making all of

Palestine part of the Roman Empire. The Jewish nation had again lost its independence by making itself weak through inner turmoil.

Judaism Under Roman Rule

The Roman invasion occurred sixty years before the birth of Jesus. The people of Jesus' era heard stories about Judea as an independent nation, and they longed for a return to this state. Some believed God would intervene, while others said they should force the foreign enemy off the land in the spirit of the Maccabean Revolt. The Roman authorities were on alert for any person among the people who would become popular enough to lead a revolt. They had a great fear of an apparent leader among the people who would identify himself as the messiah. Some of the people expected a warrior messiah who would lead them to victory and freedom from any outside ruler. Jesus had to avoid being considered the messiah lest the Roman government seek to kill him as they had killed proclaimed messiahs of the past.

In 40 BC, Rome named Herod the Great king of Samaria and Judea, but Herod had to fight to gain control of his territory in 37 BC. He eventually became king of almost all of Palestine and the land of Idumaea (Edom), just south of Judea. Because of his wide-ranging kingdom, he received the title "the Great." But even as king he was still subservient to Rome.

Herod followed the lead of other great kings of his day by imposing Hellenization on the people of his kingdom. This fact, along with the higher taxes imposed upon the people, made Herod very unpopular with Jews. Also, he came from Idumaea and was not a full-blooded Jew, which made him unwelcome to the Jews. Herod restored law and order to the land, and by the year 20 BC decided to placate the Jewish people with special favors. He began the reconstruction of the Jewish Temple in Jerusalem, a venture that would not be finished until long after the death and resurrection of Jesus. Herod is mentioned in the Scriptures as the king of Judea at the time of Jesus' birth.

At the death of Herod, the emperor of Rome divided the kingdom among Herod's three sons. The title given to the sons, each of whom took a portion of the kingdom, was "tetrarch." Philip was named tetrarch of the region just northeast of the Sea of Galilee, along with the regions known as Ituraea and Trachonitis. Herod Antipas was named tetrarch of Galilee and Perea, and Archelaus was named tetrarch of Judea and Idumaea. Philip and Herod Antipas ruled for several decades, while Archelaus proved himself incompetent and lost his position within ten years. Following Archelaus in Judea was a long line of procurators, the most famous of whom was Pilate, the procurator at Jesus' passion and death.

At the time of Jesus' birth, the Jewish people lived a life of religious freedom within the Roman Empire. The immediate religious leader of the people was the high priest. Since the religious life of the people guided almost every aspect of their daily lives, the high priest was an influential person within Judaism. This power of the high priest and the Jewish religious authorities led to jealous outbursts between the leaders of the people and the procurators. This rivalry could account for some of the debate between the religious leaders and the procurator during the passion of Jesus.

Religious Leadership

Because the religious life of the people of Jesus' day was so closely linked with their daily lives, our picture would be incomplete if we did not take a look at the religious leadership of the Jewish people. Jesus was a devout Jew who had learned, along with other children of his day, a respect for religious guidance. Despite this respect, Jesus did not hesitate to confront authority when he felt it was not true to the message of God. It was not the ordinary people of Palestine who caused problems for Jesus but the religious leaders of the day. Even the disciples believed Jesus was inviting trouble through his conflicts with religious leaders.

The Sadducees

The Sadducees could be considered the clerical group of the day. They were members of the priestly class who were wealthy and influential because of their central position in Jewish life and worship. They were the ones who served in Temple worship and took the position of mediator between God and the people. They offered sacrifices in the name of the people, and on certain occasions they entered the Holy of Holies (the inner worshiping area) in the Temple to offer incense on behalf of the people. The priesthood was held in high esteem.

The Sadducees, as members of the priestly class, tended to emphasize ceremony and liturgical law. They believed the Torah alone was the word of God and refused to accept any other books as part of Scripture. Because they accepted the Torah, the Sadducees came into conflict with Jesus over the idea of resurrection from the dead. The Sadducees refused to accept Jesus' teaching on the resurrection since they believed the Torah did not speak of it (see Matthew 22:23–33).

The Sadducees naturally supported Roman rule, not because they were happy with it, but because its stability and strength protected their authority and wealth. The idea of a revolt against Roman rule would not have been well-received by the Sadducees.

The Pharisees

Another influential group, made up of lay people, was the Pharisees. They were learned men of the day who understood and interpreted the Scriptures. The Pharisees believed the Torah and other writings of the prophets comprised the Hebrew Scriptures. Because they did not limit the Hebrew Scriptures to the Torah alone, the Pharisees often found themselves in disagreement with the Sadducees. In the Gospels, we often find Jesus in conflict with the Pharisees.

Many believe the origin of the Pharisees reaches back to the Maccabean Revolt, where they were known as the "Hasidim," or the "pious ones." The word "Pharisee" itself implies some type of separation. If we had lived during the time of Jesus, we most likely would have had little or no education. When we would meet people who had some learning, we would see them as different or separate from ourselves. The name could have implied a person who was "set apart" from the common person for the sake of interpreting the message of God. During Jesus' time the people seemed to have had a reverential fear of the Pharisees.

Although the image of the Pharisees and Sadducees presented in the Gospels seems to be one of men anxious to destroy Jesus, the Pharisees were not necessarily wicked. The Pharisees sought to preserve both the identity and the holiness of Israel through faithful observance of the law of Moses. Among their number, the Pharisees could count some sincere, dedicated men who desired to know the message of God and wanted to share it with the people.

The Scribes

There were other learned men during the time of Jesus who might or might not have belonged to the party of the Pharisees. In a society where most of the people did not learn to read or write, the scribes were held in high esteem for their learning and were called "rabbi." Many, but not all, scribes belonged to the party of the Pharisees.

Because they could read, the scribes also became the protectors and interpreters of the Scriptures for the people. A common method used in interpreting the Scriptures was to quote famous rabbis from the past. The scribes came into conflict with Jesus because he did not quote from these great rabbis but rather taught on his own authority.

The Sanhedrin

In most forms of government with which we are familiar today, there usually exists a dominant group or party, and the leader of the area or country holds an office in this body. In Judaism, the Sanhedrin was such a body. It consisted of seventy-two members drawn from among the elders, the priestly class, the Pharisees, and the scribes. The high priest presided over the assembly and held a position of great influence among the people. The Sanhedrin, or council, as it was called, governed a large part of the daily lives of the people within Judaism.

Although the country was under Roman rule, the Sanhedrin had the authority to judge cases within Judaism according to Jewish law. They made and enforced the regulations within the Jewish community and had their own police force to ensure that the people adhered to their mandates. The Gospels, perhaps reflecting early Christian prejudices, give the Sanhedrin a leading role in the trial and execution of Jesus Christ. The Gospels speak of a man named Joseph of Arimathea, a member of the council and a disciple of Jesus, who provided a burial place for the body of Jesus. The mention of his name and his concern for Jesus show that the decision of the Sanhedrin to put Jesus to death was not unanimous.

The Essenes

Among Jews at every period of history, there were those who withdrew from society to enter into deeper union with God. The Essenes were such a group within Judaism. They were a mixture of priests and lay people who believed that the Jews of their time had abandoned the spirit of the Scriptures. By withdrawing from the world that they judged to be too lax, the Essenes lived the discipline of monastic life: They shared their goods in common, prayed together, and practiced celibacy. They believed they would be prepared for the great day of salvation when it arrived.

The leader of the group, a certain "teacher of righteousness," rejected the weakness he found within the daily lives of the people. He led the Essenes in their rigid and prayerful form of life. The Essenes copied the Scriptures and wrote scrolls that would give later scholars an opportunity to learn much about the Jewish nation during the time of Jesus. The parchments, called the Dead Sea Scrolls or the Qumran Papers, were found in 1947 in caves near the Dead Sea in an area called Qumran. As mentioned in the first chapter of this book, these papers offered the world an invaluable insight into the life of the Essenes as well as important discoveries of biblical literature.

The Zealots

Every generation seems to have its fanatical terrorists who are willing to engage in battles against overwhelming odds without any apparent fear of being killed. The Zealots within Judaism fit this description well. They were a radical group of Jews who believed that God had given Judaism the right to independence and the obligation to fight for it. They knew that the Jewish nation could not rest as long as foreign rule controlled their God-given land.

The Zealots could hardly be called an organized party. They were small groups of Jews who carried out raids on government positions within Palestine. A little after the middle of the first century AD, the Zealots did form a unified cluster for a short period of time in a futile fight against the Roman army.

The messiah the Zealots awaited was a warrior messiah and king who would be sent by God to lead the nation to its rightful independence. Since God had given them the land, they expected God to help them win it back from all foreign domination. Shortly after the middle of the first century, a new hope for freedom arose when the Zealots, organized for the first time, defeated the procurator and a Syrian garrison. With the enthusiasm fired up by victory, the Zealots rallied many of the Jewish people behind them and dared to challenge the great Roman Empire. The spirit of the Maccabean Revolt seemed to be on the rise, but unfortunately Rome was not as weak as the enemies of the Maccabees. In AD 66, a Roman army entered Palestine and laid siege to the area until 70, at which time they marched into Jerusalem to destroy the city and the Temple.

With the Temple's destruction, the need for priests to offer sacrifice no longer existed, thus bringing an end to the temple priesthood (the Sadducees). The Zealots had been defeated and, except for occasional small skirmishes throughout the rest of the century, they also disappeared.

Review

✠ What were some advantages and disadvantages for the Jewish people living under Roman rule?

✠ Who were the following: the Sadducees, the Pharisees, the scribes, the Sanhedrin, the Essenes and the Zealots?

Reflection

✠ Jesus told his disciples to make disciples of all nations. How do you share God's message in your part of the world?

✠ Religion and leadership were one in the time of Jesus. How would such a situation work in our world today?

✠ Jesus was able to live in the pagan atmosphere of Rome yet remain faithful to the one true God without confronting the pagan authorities. How should Christians confront governments that are helpful in some cases but hurtful to certain areas?

II. UNDERSTANDING THE MESSAGE

When Jesus asked Peter who he thought Jesus was, Peter answered, "You are the Messiah, the Son of the living God" (Matthew 16:16). Jesus commends Peter but adds that he received this revelation from God. It came as a gift of faith, not through human reasoning.

Jesus the Messiah

Because of the advantage of viewing the Old Testament through the eyes of the resurrection, Christians can more easily understand the true meaning of "messiah." For the people of Jesus' day, however, a true understanding of the awaited Messiah came slowly.

A New King and Leader

The people of Israel looked back to the days when their nation was a strong, independent kingdom that bred fear in the hearts of surrounding nations. The most revered king of Israel's past glory was David. In later centuries, people believed God would send a savior to free the people from foreign domination and that this savior would come from the Davidic line. This expected savior would be called the Messiah.

Recognizing Jesus as the Messiah

After the resurrection of Jesus, his disciples recognized him as the true Messiah, and they began to clarify their thinking concerning the true nature of the word. He was not a warrior king who would bring material freedom to the people but rather a spiritual king who would bring eternal salvation and new life to the people. This new life came to the people through the death, resurrection, and ascension of Jesus, and it is properly through his resurrection from the dead that Jesus could be called the Messiah. "Christ" is a Greek translation of "Messiah." Another term for Messiah is "the Anointed One." Used properly, our Savior's title is "Jesus the Christ."

Early in their travels, Jesus' disciples had difficulty understanding his message, but they gradually began to suspect that he was indeed the long-awaited Messiah. Then the Roman authorities put Jesus to death, as they did with self-proclaimed messiahs in the past. The confusion of Jesus' disciples is best described in Luke's Gospel as two of Jesus' disciples, walking on the road to Emmaus, are joined by Jesus, whom they do not recognize, and they explain the things that are bothering them.

> "The things that happened to Jesus the Nazarene, who was a prophet mighty in deed and word before God and all the people, how our chief priests and rulers both handed him over to a sentence of death and crucified him. But we were hoping that he would be the one to redeem Israel; and besides all this, it is now the third day since this took place. Some women from our group, however, have astounded us: they were at the tomb early in the morning and did not find his body; they came back and reported that they had indeed seen a vision of angels who announced that he was alive" (Luke 24:19–23).

With Jesus' resurrection, the disciples' understanding of him changed dramatically, shedding new light on his life, his message, and his death. A major consequence of this new understanding was the development of the New Testament.

The New Testament is not a biography of Jesus, not a collection of diaries written by the companions of Jesus, and not the imaginative creation of several men who wrote after the resurrection of Jesus. It is the result of a struggle of Jesus' disciples to understand, preach, and preserve the message of Jesus Christ in light of his resurrection. What the disciples also learned was the unimaginable truth that Jesus the Christ was also the Son of God.

The Son of God

The understanding of the early Church concerning the divinity of Jesus developed gradually. The later the date of each Gospel, the more developed is the presentation and understanding of Jesus' divinity. The Gospel of John, written at the end of the first century, has a much more developed presentation of the divinity of Jesus than the Gospels of Mark, Matthew, and Luke, which were written some twenty to thirty-five years earlier. John introduces his Gospel by identifying Jesus as the "Word" before the creation of the world, and he writes: "In the beginning was the Word, and the Word was with God, and the Word was God" (John 1:1).

The early Christians preached that Jesus Christ was the Son of God and one with God the Father. Paul the Apostle reveals that Jesus is God when he writes: "He is the image of the invisible God, the firstborn of all creation. For in him were created all things in heaven and on earth, the visible and invisible, whether thrones or dominations or principalities or powers; all things were created through him and for him" (Colossians 1:15–16). When Philip asks Jesus to show them the Father, meaning God, Jesus answers, "Whoever has seen me has seen the Father" (John 14:9). When Jesus comes out of the water after his baptism by John the Baptist, a voice from heaven proclaims, "You are my beloved Son; with you I am well pleased" (Mark 1:11). The early disciples accepted faith in Jesus' divinity within a short period after his resurrection as they reflected on his life and message.

Developing the Message

The disciples in the Gospel of Mark are portrayed as men slow to understand Jesus. Even after witnessing the miracles of Jesus, the disciples lacked understanding. At one point, Jesus had to say to them in frustration, "Do you still not understand" (Mark 8:21)? When Jesus was arrested in the Garden of Gethsemane, "they all left him and fled" (Mark 14:50). If we knew as little about Jesus as the disciples did at the time, we also might have panicked and joined the mad rush to get out of the Garden.

Once the disciples realized that Jesus actually rose from the dead, they had to do some serious reflection. On the day of Jesus' ascension, the disciples returned to the upper room, where they pondered day after day the events that had taken place. We can imagine them engaged in heavy discussion, shaking their heads, pacing the floor, recalling the words of Jesus—trying to put it all together in their minds and hearts.

Finally, on Pentecost, under the influence of the Holy Spirit, the pieces had fallen into place. The message and person of Jesus Christ began to have deeper meaning for the disciples. Now they understood, and once they did, they were ready to share the Good News with others. Little did they realize when they left that upper room that they were about to unleash a message that would change the lives of billions of people for centuries to come.

The key to the disciples' understanding of Jesus and his message was the resurrection. Once they understood that Jesus had been raised as he predicted, they were like people who suddenly complete a jigsaw puzzle after putting the final piece in its proper place. As they pondered Jesus' message, they looked back through the eyes of the resurrection to see the meaning of his life and his word. Everything looked so very different once Jesus had been raised from the dead. The disciples recalled the message contained in the Hebrew Scriptures and the promises God made to the Chosen People of Israel, and they understood the Old Testament promises in a way they had never dreamed. They were now prepared to share Jesus' message with the world. When they began, the New Testament did not yet exist, but their preaching about Jesus' life and message eventually found its way into the written message.

Preaching to All Nations

The sharing of the early message of Jesus Christ began in the land of Judea. The early followers of Jesus would enter the synagogues and preach about Jesus Christ, the Son of God, who fulfilled the promises God made to Israel. To their surprise, those who believed in Jesus as the Christ began to find they were not welcome in the synagogues. The disciples of Jesus expected Jews to recognize that Jesus was the Christ and to become his followers. They believed the Jews were the Chosen People and that the prophets spoke of the Messiah coming through Judaism. The early disciples never spoke of beginning a new form of religion. They referred to themselves as "the Way," meaning that a new path for the Jewish people was built on the old. Now that the promise of the coming of the Messiah was fulfilled, Jews would certainly recognize him.

Gentile Converts

Some missionaries took the message outside Palestine and began preaching to pagans, whom Jews called "gentiles." A gentile was any man, woman, or child who did not belong to the Jewish nation. Jews looked down on gentiles and would refer to them in a derogatory manner by calling them by the name of some lowly animal. To Jews, gentiles were pagans who did not have the gift of Mosaic law to guide them and who often believed in many gods. To the surprise of everyone, a large number of gentiles accepted the message of Jesus Christ, and many turned to Christianity.

Apostle to the Gentiles

Paul was the great apostle to the gentiles. One of the early conflicts within Christianity arose over the problem of burdening the gentiles with Jewish law as found in the Pentateuch. Paul believed Jesus Christ had done away with many of the prescriptions of the Jewish law for these new converts, while others believed that Christianity, because it had its roots in Judaism, should continue with these prescriptions. A Church gathering in Jerusalem around the middle of the first century (later called the First Council of Jerusalem) declared the gentiles free of certain Jewish prescriptions. This opened the way for even greater missionary activity among gentiles.

Throughout the Old Testament, many Israelites had been hoping for the arrival of the Messiah. The promises God made had kept alive a hope that soon salvation would come. For those who accepted Christ, the message had finally reached its fulfillment. But with the decision at Jerusalem allowing freedom from some Jewish traditions for new converts, they might have believed all was being lost. The house was being turned over to others. Jewish converts to Christianity put up strong resistance to the setting aside of Jewish traditions.

Today Christians take for granted the fact that our traditions and customs differ to some degree from those of the Jewish religion. If Paul had not fought for the sake of the gentiles, we might still be practicing Jewish traditions. Paul suffered a great deal of pain due to the Judaizers who did not agree with the Council of Jerusalem. "Judaizers" referred to Jewish converts to Christ who believed they had to enforce the need to remain faithful to Jewish laws and customs. They undermined Paul's work to the point that he was completely ineffective with the Jewish audience. Because of Paul's persistence, Christianity, although from Jewish roots, had taken on a different set of traditions—some closely linked with Judaism, some completely new to Christianity.

Paul and other missionaries of his day would enter a village or town during their missionary journeys and set up a Christian community, known as the Church. Although we often use "church" to refer to a building, "Church" refers to a community of people. Through baptism, we are the Church. Once missionaries established a Church community, they would move on to do the same in another area.

The Canon of the New Testament

A group of schoolchildren laughed when a teacher told them that people at one time thought the earth was flat. These children, like each of us, had learned from a very young age that the earth was round, and they had accepted it as truth. To think otherwise would appear ridiculous to these children.

We have many such facts in our minds that were planted early and grew as we grew. One of these facts, for many Christians, was that there was a New Testament, inspired by God, and that specific books made up the New Testament. We might not have been able to name the books, but we knew they were there, safely tucked away between the covers. They belonged to the New Testament as surely as the earth was round.

Just as people had to struggle and take risks to prove the world was round, so others had to struggle to establish which books belonged to the New Testament. In the early Church, there were many writers who tried to put the meaning of the life and message of Jesus Christ into a book or letter. Some writers faithfully reflected the teaching of the early Church while others were affected by outside influences that were contrary to the message. Under the guidance of the Holy Spirit, members of the early Church community began to make use of certain books or letters while rejecting others. The writers themselves never realized they had written inspired books, but the early Church began to look to certain books as the Christian Scriptures.

By the end of the first century, most of the books of the New Testament were written, and by the end of the second century, most of the books were widely accepted as written under the inspiration of the Holy Spirit. By the middle of the second century, Christians began to quote the books of the New Testament, giving it the same authority as the Old Testament. It was not until the middle of the sixth century that the present list of writings was unanimously accepted as true Christian Scriptures.

In the sixteenth century, the well-known Council of Trent established the official canon of the New Testament. It consists of twenty-seven books, which include four Gospels, the Acts of the Apostles, twenty-one letters, and the Book of Revelation. As we read through the New Testament today, we may not be aware of the struggle involved in defining the true books of the collection. To be able to point to these books with the assurance that they are the word of God for all Christians is an assurance that should not be taken for granted.

Jewish Feasts

As Christians, we celebrate feasts that remind us of certain events in Jesus' life. Examples of such feasts are Christmas and Easter. As United States citizens, we also celebrate certain festival days that are important to us as a country. For example, we celebrate Independence Day on the fourth of July. Since the Jewish people had their religion so closely linked with their daily life, their national feasts were always religious in nature. These feasts often recalled past events in the life of the Israelite nation and the part that God played in each event.

Passover

A major feast within Judaism of Jesus' day was Passover. This celebration commemorated the occasion when God freed the Israelites from slavery in Egypt. On this day, the people would bring a lamb to the temple to be sacrificed by the priests. This recalled the story of the Israelites who, on the evening of their escape from Egypt, killed a lamb and painted its blood on their doorposts. The angel of death passed over those homes with this blood on the doorpost and went on to kill all the firstborn among the Egyptians. Jews still gather together for a ceremonial supper on the night of Passover, remembering how God led them from slavery to the Promised Land and freedom.

Pentecost

Another important feast within Judaism was that of Pentecost. This commemorated the time when the Israelites, fifty days after leaving Egypt, received the law from God through the mediation of Moses on Mount Sinai. "Pentecost" comes from the Greek root meaning "fifty." This event was also referred to as the Feast of Weeks, and it was celebrated at harvest time.

Hanukkah and Other Feasts

Among the other feasts was that of Hanukkah, which commemorated the rededication of the temple of Judas Maccabeus. The observance of the Jewish New Year, the Day of Atonement (Yom Kippur), and the Solemnity of Tabernacles were three feasts that came close together. On the Day of Atonement, the people would atone for their sins by fasting, ritual bathing, prayer, and temple sacrifice. The feast of tabernacles apparently commemorated the time the Israelites spent in tents (tabernacles) in the desert.

Review

✠ How did the disciples come to the conclusion that Jesus was the promised Messiah?

✠ Who are the Judaizers and gentiles, and what issues in the early Church affected both groups?

✠ How did the canon of the New Testament develop?

✠ What are some of the major feasts within Judaism?

Reflection

✠ When Peter declared that Jesus was the Christ, Jesus responded that Peter received this knowledge as a gift of faith. What gifts of faith have you received?

✠ The resurrection of Jesus helped Jesus' disciples understand the message of his life. How does an understanding of Jesus as the Christ and the Son of God affect your life?

✠ The New Testament gives us insight into the life and message of Jesus the Christ. How has the New Testament, as the inspired word of God, helped you to understand God's dealings with creation?

CHAPTER FIVE

The World of the Writer

I. WRITING THE NEW TESTAMENT

At times, when Paul could not return to visit the Churches he had founded, he would write them a letter and send it to them with one of his companions. Paul's letters show the fondness of a founder. He loved the Churches he founded as a parent would love a child. He would encourage them, rebuke them, instruct them, and warn them against false prophets. On a rare occasion, such as his Letter to the Romans, Paul would write to a Church founded by someone else, but it was one that he longed to visit.

Letters (Epistles)

The letters of Paul are among the first writings of the New Testament. He wrote his early letters more than twenty years after the resurrection of Jesus. Paul had secretaries who would write his letters as he dictated them, and these secretaries would often be mentioned in the letters. The epistles of Paul, as well as the letters of James, Peter, John, and Jude, make up the collection of letters in the New Testament.

Another custom in the early Church was one that we might consider illegal today. A letter writer might use the name of some well-known figure to give that letter more authority. Although many letters of the New Testament are attributed to Paul, he did not write some of them. A writer would feel free to use Paul's name on a letter if the writer felt the letter reflected Paul's thinking. When Paul and others wrote the letters found in the New Testament, they had no idea those letters would become part of the Christian Scriptures. They simply wrote each letter with the hope of helping the community for which it was intended.

There are twenty-one letters in the New Testament, although some could not strictly be called letters. Some sound like sermons or treatises on specific subjects. Whatever we call them, these letters make up the bulk of the New Testament.

The letters many scholars attribute to Paul are usually named after the community or person to whom they are addressed, although there is some question about the true identity of the recipients. The names given to these letters are: Romans, 1 and 2 Corinthians, Galatians, Ephesians, Philippians, Colossians, 1 and 2 Thessalonians, 1 and 2 Timothy, Titus, and Philemon. Letters not attributed to Paul have the names of other apostles or writers to whom they are attributed, although there is some question about the real authors of these letters. These are James, 1 and 2 Peter, Jude, and 1—3 John. The author of Hebrews is unknown.

The Gospels

As missionary activities spread throughout the world, the need for some written message about Jesus became apparent. The people who had lived with Jesus were dying, and the early Church recognized the need to preserve the message before the last of the witnesses to Jesus' life passed away. As the message spread farther from the land of its source and began to reach territories unfamiliar with Judean ways, the roots had to be protected. Christianity, like Judaism, was a religion that had developed a history. That history had to be preserved.

More than thirty-five years after the resurrection of Jesus, an author identified as Mark wrote the first Gospel. In some ways, the author must have been a unique person. In order to write the Gospel, he had to invent a new type of literature. Until Mark wrote down the message of Jesus, no one had developed the type of writing called a Gospel.

The author of the Gospel of Mark gathered together some of the stories of Jesus' life, the sayings of Jesus, his miracle stories, and his passion narrative, and presented them in an orderly fashion. What he wrote was not a biography in the strictest sense of the word but a result of the reflection of the early Church community on the life of Jesus. Mark's concern was not to present an exact account of Jesus' daily ministry but an attempt to present the message about Jesus, that is, the meaning behind his life, his person, and his teachings.

Authors identified as Matthew and Luke used Mark's format as an outline for their Gospels and added other sources. These authors wrote more than fifty years after the resurrection of Jesus. Finally, an author identified as John wrote a Gospel almost seventy years after the resurrection. As with the letters of Paul, none of these writers realized their books would eventually become part of the Christian Scriptures.

The Acts of the Apostles

The Acts of the Apostles tells us how the early Church developed and shared the message of Jesus. The book describes the early struggles of the community in trying to understand its own identity. Acts follows the missionary activities of such great leaders as Peter and Paul. The book not only has value in telling us what the early Church did after the resurrection and ascension of Jesus, but it also tells us that Jesus was still acting through his followers. The Book of Acts follows immediately after the Gospels in the present structure of the New Testament.

The book stresses the activity of the Holy Spirit in the life of the Church. On the Jewish Feast of Pentecost, Jews crowded into Jerusalem from throughout the Roman Empire. In a dramatic rendering, the Acts of the Apostles describes a world-shaking event, namely the coming of the Holy Spirit upon the disciples of Jesus. The author of Acts describes a visible infusion of the Holy Spirit on Jesus' followers as though tongues of fire settled on them. The impact of the gift of the Spirit upon the followers of Jesus was so intense that they immediately set out to face the very people who put Jesus to death. The activity of the Holy Spirit not only enables a person to preach the message, it also opens the hearts and minds of the listeners to hear the message. As a result of Peter's first day of preaching, as related in the Acts of the Apostles, many people "who accepted his message were baptized" (2:41).

The Book of Revelation

The Book of Revelation was a message for Christians undergoing persecution and was meant to encourage them to remain firm in the midst of suffering and evil. Those familiar with the Old Testament Scriptures would recognize the use and inferences of apocalyptic language. It was a type of literature familiar to many of the early Christians but unclear to the Roman mind. The Book of Revelation makes use of symbolic language that is found in Old Testament apocalyptic works and other Jewish writings during the centuries immediately before and after the coming of Jesus.

The Book of Revelation is also known as the Apocalypse because of its use of apocalyptic language. The basic message of Revelation is the same as all apocalyptic writing, namely that evil has power only as long as God allows such power, but in the end, God will overcome evil and triumph.

Revelation begins in a letter format but soon switches to the apocalyptic style that will be understood by many Christians but not comprehended by the persecutors themselves. The Book of Revelation is the last book found in the New Testament.

The Cultural and Political Environment

When we try to understand the history of major events in the world—for example, the Protestant Reformation—we must first try to understand what the world was like at the time of the Reformation. If the world situation had been the same in the sixteenth century as it is today, we possibly would have an entirely different outcome to the Reformation. The same holds true for the New Testament. If it had been written today, we would most likely have a far different type of book than we have from the writers of the first century after Christ. In the same way, if the New Testament had been preached or written four centuries earlier, it would have taken much longer to spread throughout the known world. The environment, shaped by history, had a very large influence upon the spread of the New Testament.

Greek Language

Before missionaries begin to speak about Christ to people of other countries, they must naturally first learn the language of the people with whom they are speaking. When the books of the New Testament were being written, most people in that part of the world spoke Greek. Thanks to the zeal of Alexander the Great and those who followed, the Greek language had become the basic language of the empire. Even under the domination of Rome, "the world" continued to speak Greek.

In the early days of missionary activity, missionaries could enter an area and begin to teach the people in Greek without any language barrier. The Hebrew Bible had been translated into Greek several centuries earlier, and most Jews outside Jerusalem were more familiar with the Greek version of the Bible than with the Hebrew version. This enabled missionaries to quote from the Old Testament in a language familiar to everyone, and it further enabled them to show how Jesus was the fulfillment of the Old Testament promise.

New Testament writings spread rapidly due to this common language, especially to those outside Jerusalem. The many Jews who had lived outside Jerusalem since the Diaspora became a major target of Christian preaching and conversion. Without the common Greek language, it is difficult to conceive how Christianity could have spread as quickly as it did.

Stability of the Empire

With most of the known world under Roman domination, traveling was less dangerous due to Roman patrols on the roads and on the sea. Rome also built roads that made it easier for travel. Christian preachers could more easily move from one area to another in spreading their message. Merchants and traders who converted to Christianity also became evangelizers as they passed along the message of Jesus in large centers of trade. People were always anxious to hear news from other ports, and the traders were the ones who often brought this news.

Persecution

Persecution was a surprising element in the spread of Christianity. When Romans and Judeans alike began to persecute the early Christians, many were forced to flee to other areas beyond Judea, and they brought their faith with them. An early persecution by the religious leaders in Jerusalem forced the Greek-speaking converts to Christ to flee to areas like Samaria and further north to Antioch. In doing this, they had greater contact with the gentiles, who accepted faith in Christ more readily than the strict Judeans who believed that Christians were contaminating Judaism and causing God to punish Israel.

With the destruction of the Temple and Jerusalem, Christianity had to take an even closer look at its mission as distinct from Judaism. By this time, many gentiles had been converted to Christianity, and their reliance upon the holy city was not as important as it was to Jewish converts. When the city was destroyed, Christianity became less identified with Judaism and began to be seen as a religion distinct from Judaism. Without ties to the holy city and the Temple, Christianity moved even closer to the gentile world.

When Bible scholars study the Scriptures to discover its message, they look not only at the material presented, but they try to discover the original material before the author made use of it, what the author did with the material, and why one author would present the same material in a fashion different from other authors. They look, in other words, at the "world of the writer" to understand the original material better. The results of the studies of these Scripture scholars fall under three categories: (a) redaction criticism, (b) form criticism, and (c) source criticism.

Redaction Criticism

Before someone writes a book, he or she must first gather the material. Then the author must determine the audience for which the book will be written and identify the aim of the book. These two factors determine the book's format. Some books are simply an adaptation of sources compiled to present a specific message to a specific audience. The process that prepares sources in such a way that they are ready for publication is called "redaction." To redact, according to the dictionary, means to edit or to prepare for publication. Redaction criticism is a study of the process used by the authors of the Gospels in the preparation of their resource material for publication.

Teaching a Message

The value of redaction criticism is that it helps us understand more clearly the lesson the authors wished to teach in using their resources in a certain way. For instance, Matthew pictures Jesus going up a mountainside to preach the Beatitudes (5:1), while Luke pictures Jesus coming down the mountain to a level stretch of land (6:17). From the context of the Gospel of Matthew, we learn that the author adapted his material in such a way as to show a relationship between the people of Israel and the followers of Jesus. Just as God gave a new law to the people of Israel on a mountain, so Jesus gave a new law to his followers, the New Israel, on a mountain. By understanding the manner in which the author of the Gospel of Matthew used his material, we can more fully understand the message he wished to teach.

The Events of Jesus' Life

Redaction criticism also recognizes that the authors of the Gospels were not simply editors who arranged their material in a historical perspective. They were also theologians who arranged their material according to the message they wished to teach. Even if they wanted to write a biography about Jesus, they would not have been able to do so. Their resources came from the many forms used in the early preaching rather than from their own personal eyewitness to the life of Jesus. They wanted to write about Jesus the Christ, the Son of God who had been raised from the dead.

In stating that the authors of the Gospels did not write a biography, we must not give the impression that they invented the events of Jesus' life. Those events form a major part of the outline of the Gospels, although they might not have happened in the order and with the exact details given. We can learn much about the life of Jesus from the Gospels.

Audience

The audience for whom they were writing influenced the Gospels' authors to a great degree. What were the needs and the questions of this audience? The author of the Gospel of Matthew, for instance, was writing for Jewish converts to Christianity. Thus Matthew portrayed Jesus as the fulfillment of the Old Testament promises that were familiar to the Jewish audience. The author of the Gospel of Mark, with a different audience in mind, would not place the same importance on the Old Testament. Knowledge of the audience helps us understand the message the author wished to share.

Situation of the Church

Another influence upon the authors of the Gospels was the situation in the Church at the time of the writing. What influences inside and outside the Church were affecting the audience when the Gospel was written? If we were to write a book that would help U.S. citizens live a good life in the modern world, we would most likely have written a different book fifty years ago than we would write now. The audience for whom the authors wrote were living in history, and their historical situation deeply affected the message they needed to hear.

In summary, the authors of the Gospels made use of events from Jesus' life as well as the many preaching methods used in the early Church. The audience for whom they wrote and the situation in the Church at the time of the writing highly influenced the major emphasis of their message. This knowledge of the sources and influences that gave us the final written Gospels helps us understand the author's message with greater precision. This is the value of redaction criticism.

Review

✠ What is the importance of the letters of the New Testament, and how many can you name?

✠ What do we mean when we say the Gospels are not biographies of Jesus?

✠ How did the Greek influence and stability of the Roman Empire help early Christianity?

✠ What is redaction criticism, and why is it important?

Reflection

✠ The Gospels are a result of a faith reflection of the early Church on the life and message of Jesus. How does this knowledge help you in your spiritual development?

✠ Common language and travel conditions helped the spread of Christianity during the time of the early Church. Do you believe Christianity would have spread as quickly today with our modern conditions?

✠ The writers of the Gospels were influenced by (a) the events in Jesus' life, (b) the condition of the Church at the time of the writing, and (c) the audience for whom the Gospels were written. Do any of these categories affect our interpretation of the Gospels today?

II. THE SOURCES OF THE NEW TESTAMENT

When we read an obituary of someone who recently died, we expect to read about the good qualities of that person and his or her loving relationships. An obituary is a type of writing used to summarize the good qualities and works of a person. The person who composed the obituary may have had to call some elderly relatives to ask where "Dad" worked after he graduated from high school seventy years earlier. Someone may disagree with a place of work found in the obituary and ask, "Who was the source of that information." In the obituary, we find a type of literary form and a need for sources. The writing of the New Testament involved both types.

Form Criticism

When we read a newspaper, our minds immediately attune themselves to the specific type of writing we are reading. We know that the first page of a newspaper usually gives factual information, telling us what is happening in the world. If we read on the first page that a gang injured a man by beating him, we would read this as bad news. When we read an advertisement on the second page telling us that a "miracle" pill will rid us of arthritis, we know that advertisements often make exaggerated claims, so we do not rush out to buy the pill. When we read on the sports page that one football team beat another, we do not expect the winning club to be arrested for violence. "Beat" has a different meaning on the sports page than it does on the first page. All of these works are different forms of writing. No one has to tell us how to interpret each type of writing. We automatically adapt to each form.

When we attempt to read literature written many centuries ago in a culture different from our own, we could make the mistake of believing that the form is the same form of writing that we use today. The Scriptures are composed of poems, hymns, letters, wisdom sayings, miracle stories, and myths. The study whereby Scripture scholars try to identify these various forms of writing is called "form" criticism.

In our study of the New Testament Gospels, we must strive to get behind the written word to the message as it was first preached. We mentioned earlier that the message of the "Good News" fell into clusters or categories of writings that were used for preaching a common message. A name given to these clusters by Scripture scholars is "pericopes" (per-ICK-o-pees). They fall under such categories as (a) pronouncement stories, (b) sayings of Jesus, (c) parables, (d) miracle stories, and (e) stories about Jesus. These categories list the specific forms used in preaching the message. Another expression used for the preached message is the "oral tradition."

Pronouncement Stories

When we wish to make a statement that is important, we make use of various methods to draw attention to it. We can tell the audience we have something important to say. We can shout when we reach the important part, or we can couch our important lesson in an interesting story. A pronouncement story makes use of this last method. A pronouncement story is a short narrative that has as its goal the presentation of some major pronouncement. The narrative is often a conflict story that builds toward the important statement. The message is often general enough to fit more than one story or situation.

An example of a pronouncement story is found in Mark 2:23–28, when the author tells of Jesus' disciples plucking grain on the Sabbath. The Sabbath was the most sacred day of the week for Jews, and they had strict rules about work on this day. When the Pharisees saw the disciples plucking grain on the Sabbath, they complained to Jesus that his disciples were performing a type of work on the Sabbath. Jesus answered their complaint with a pronouncement that the Sabbath was made for humanity, and not humanity for the Sabbath (Mark 2:27).

Sayings of Jesus

When we quote someone, we often omit the events that surround the statement quoted. The reason is that we are simply interested in what a person had to say rather than the events. When we speak of the "sayings of Jesus," we are speaking about a collection of sayings that are not placed in any type of narrative format. They are simply quotes from Jesus' life.

The preachers of the early Church had many collections of these sayings of Jesus. Many were individual utterances of Jesus that the preachers strung together according to a given theme. An example of such individual sayings put together in this way may be found in Mark 8:34–38, where Jesus invites anyone to come with him by denying himself and taking up the cross. This is followed by a statement about the futility of gaining the whole world and losing one's soul. A third statement, following immediately, speaks about the outcome in store for the person who is ashamed of Jesus Christ. Each of these statements is a saying of Jesus, most likely made at different times but brought together by those who preached the message due to a similarity of the theme.

Another example of a collection of the various sayings of Jesus is found in the Gospel of Matthew, where the author gathers the sayings of Jesus to shape his Sermon on the Mount (chapters 5—7). These chapters in Matthew show the writer's unique way of collecting Jesus' sayings.

Parables

The best way to teach a lesson to an audience that has no books is to tell a story. The point of the story then becomes the point that a person wishes to teach. When we speak of parables, we are referring to the stories Jesus told. When Jesus told these stories, he made comparisons with experiences from the lives of his listeners. When Jesus wanted to speak of the kingdom of heaven, he compared it to something familiar. For instance, Jesus said the kingdom of heaven "is like a mustard seed that, when it is sown in the ground, is the smallest of all seeds on the earth" (Mark 4:31). Then he told his story. A parable could be a lengthy narrative such as the story of the son who abandoned his inheritance and returned home to his forgiving father (Luke 15:11–32), or it could be as short as a few lines, such as the parable about a person who put new wine into old wineskins (Mark 2:22).

A parable is properly a story with a single theme and a single message. The point of the story usually comes at the end. Jesus added surprise endings to his parables that brought the messages home with more force. The stories themselves had some elements of surprise that made the listener pay special attention. What shepherd would leave ninety-nine sheep to the possible ravages of wolves just to save one sheep? What father would forgive a son who had taken advantage of the family as did the prodigal son? The practice of using parables to get across a single message came from the Old Testament, and it was more familiar to those steeped in Old Testament traditions.

Allegory

When the message of Jesus began to spread outside Palestine, the parables gradually became allegories. Where a parable has a single message that is usually reached at the end, an allegory gives meaning to each detail of a story. When Jesus told the story of the sower who went out to sow the seed, he developed the story by having some seed fall among thorns, on stone, or on the roadway. The seed that fell upon good soil brought an overwhelming harvest. The message Jesus wished to share in this parable was that those who accept the word of God in their lives will produce an abundant harvest.

During the preaching of this parable by the early Church, it gradually became an allegory. The seed took on the meaning of the word of God, while the thorns, the rock, and the roadway all took on the meaning of some worldly weakness or obstacle to the reception of the message. Those who received the word of God were like the good soil that gave an abundant harvest. Each detail of the story had a meaning and, with this change, the story actually became an allegory instead of a parable in its strictest sense.

Many parables became allegories as the early preachers interpreted the message for their listeners. When the writers of the Gospels made use of these parables in their writings, they found many parables had already become allegories, and they used them in this form. Since the parables were preached individually or with other short parables, the early preachers did not fit them into a historical context. The Gospel writers chose the appropriate places for parables in the Gospel narrative.

Miracle Stories

A person with miraculous powers will always draw large crowds as long as there are people suffering from some sickness or disease and in need of healing. Jesus certainly drew large crowds as he healed people of their various illnesses. Without a doubt, Jesus was a miracle worker.

The messages conveyed by many of the miracle stories in the Gospels came from knowledge gained by the early community after the resurrection of Jesus. Some of the miracle tales grew into more elaborate stories through use among these first followers. Under the guidance of the Holy Spirit, the early community wanted to share the true message of Jesus, namely that he was the Christ, the Son of God. The purpose of the miracle stories was to point to this revelation. Scripture scholars believe Jesus was indeed a miracle worker, but they hesitate to accept all the miracles precisely as they are reported in the Gospels. None of the Scripture scholars dispute the message toward which these miracles point.

The miracle stories were usually preached according to a specific format. The first part of the miracle story ordinarily described the condition of the person in need of healing. The person was blind, possessed by an evil spirit, crippled, and so on. The second part of the miracle story told how Jesus performed the miracle. He would touch the person, command the evil spirits to leave the person, pray over the person, or give some type of word that would heal the person. The third part of the miracle story showed some type of reaction to the miracle. The people around were astounded, confused, made to believe, or even inclined to put Jesus to death.

The early preachers apparently preached about the individual miracles of Jesus. Some editors may have gathered them into a collection of stories at a later time. Like the other forms used for preaching, the miracle stories were not preached within a particular historical context. The later writers placed the stories in the Gospels where they taught the message that the writer wished to emphasize.

Stories About Jesus' Life

Besides the four patterns just given, some stories do not fit under any of these categories. There are the stories that tell of the infancy of Jesus, the choosing of his apostles, the temptations of Jesus in the desert, and a list of other events that were part of the preaching of the early Church. These stories do not end with any specific type of pronouncement, although they do give a further message about Jesus and the people who surrounded Jesus during his ministry. The Gospel writers also drew upon these stories in structuring their works.

Source Criticism

When someone offers us new information in a serious discussion, we tend to ask for the source of that information: "Where did you get that?" If we find that the source is reliable, we accept the information without further question.

Original Source

When we speak of "source criticism" with respect to the Gospels, we are speaking about the desire to get to the original source of information, what it said, and how it was used. In attempting to do this, scholars ran into problems. Many sources used in the Gospels came from the preaching of the early Church community. Much of the material was not written down until it appeared in the Gospels, or if it was written down, most of the early sources have never been found.

Understanding the Exact Content

Although we have already spoken of the various forms of preaching the message of Jesus, we can only speculate on the exact content of these sources. We must work backward from the Gospels. As Scripture scholars study the Gospels, they try to isolate the original form of the information contained in it. When they do this, they are then able to speculate on why the author used this form in this particular context. In doing this, we are able to come closer to the message the Gospel writer wished to share.

The Synoptic Gospels

When two people agree on something, there is an expression that says they see "eye to eye." A free translation of "synoptic" could have that same meaning. It comes from a Greek word meaning "seeing together," and it is applied to the Gospels of Mark, Matthew, and Luke. They have so many similarities that they actually seem to be looking at the message of Jesus together. In many areas, they agree word for word with one another. A "synoptic problem" occurs when scholars try to discover why these three Gospels have so much in common yet also have differences.

Mark as a Source

If the Gospel of Mark was lost, it could be reproduced almost entirely from the Gospels of Matthew and Luke. Most scholars agree that the Gospel of Mark was written first, and that the Gospels of Matthew and Luke used the Gospel of Mark as a source. The author of the Gospel of Matthew copied almost all of the Gospel of Mark, while the author of the Gospel of Luke copied about half of Mark's Gospel. At times, they copied an episode from the Gospel of Mark with little or no change, while at other times they would adapt the passages to fit their message.

The Sayings of Jesus as a Source

This is not the only aspect of the synoptic problem. Besides those passages that Matthew and Luke have used from Mark, they also have passages in common with each other that are not found in the Gospel of Mark. This means the authors of the Gospels of Matthew and Luke not only had Mark as a common source, but they also had another common source unknown to Mark. The fact that the authors of Matthew and Luke often agree in style and in the use of specific words would indicate that this common source known only to them must have been a written source rather than a preached source. These passages found only in the Gospels of Matthew and Luke consist mainly of the sayings of Jesus and his parables. The title given to this source is "Q," which comes from the first letter of the German word "Quelle," which means "source." Although Mark had no knowledge of this "Q" source, it could easily have predated the writing of his Gospel.

The Oral Source

A third ingredient of the synoptic problem comes in the form of passages found in the Gospel of Matthew alone, or in the Gospel of Luke alone. Each writer seems to have a third source unknown to the other. This source could have been oral or a written source. For simplicity, Scripture scholars refer to the source known only to Matthew as the "M" source, and the source known only to Luke as the "L" source.

At this point, it might be well to present the synoptic problem in the following manner:

1. Mark
2. Mark + Q + M = Matthew
3. Mark + Q + L = Luke

The Value of Studying the Synoptic Sources

The value of the study of the synoptic Gospels is that it enables us to understand the Gospels of Matthew and Luke better. The manner in which Matthew and Luke make use of their common sources gives us a deeper insight into the messages of their Gospels. We can understand their more subtle teachings by studying the manner in which they used and adapted their sources to their message. Because we do not have a written collection of the sources used by Mark, we are unable to compare the sources with the manner in which Mark used them in his Gospel.

In John, a much later Gospel, we find speeches of Jesus and narratives not found in the synoptic Gospels. Although there are some similarities, the Gospel of John makes use of other sources not known to Matthew, Mark, or Luke. For this reason, the Gospel of John is not considered one of the synoptic Gospels.

Review

✠ What do we mean by form criticism?

✠ What do we mean by the following: (a) pronouncement stories, (b) sayings of Jesus, (c) parables?

✠ What do we mean by source criticism? How do we solve the synoptic problem with source criticism?

Reflection

✠ When Moses tells the Israelites to fix God's words in their hearts, he is telling them to make God's words the guide for their life. How are you fixing God's word in your heart?

✠ The source of the Gospels comes from the many forms used in preaching the Gospel in the early Church. What is the value of knowing the various literary forms used in the formation of the Gospels?

✠ The fact that the Gospels of Matthew and Luke used Mark as a source gives us a greater insight into the message of these Gospels. What is the spiritual value of having three Gospels that are similar in some areas and different in others?

CHAPTER SIX

Spreading the Message

I. UNDERSTANDING JESUS

By studying the history, culture, and values that surround people in a particular society, we can catch a glimpse of the type of person such a society would likely produce. Jesus was a devout Jew, deeply involved in the religious history of his people, and faithfully responsive to the demands of faith in his daily life. As a child, he probably sat and learned at the feet of a scholarly rabbi, gained a deep love and reverence for the Scriptures, felt frustration at the lack of Jewish political independence, worshiped regularly in the synagogues, and loved to visit the holy city of Jerusalem and the Temple. As an adult, Jesus challenged some of the contemporary thinking that clashed with his understanding of the Hebrew Scriptures.

If we had lived in a town near Nazareth, we might never have heard about the young Jesus. If we had played with him as a child, we might never have noticed anything different about him. Jesus was not a little child turning clay birds into living birds. Jesus was a child who lived as normal a life as the child next door. As a baby, he cried when he was hungry. As a young boy, he may not have been the best athlete in town. The villagers had become so familiar with the ordinary Jesus that they could not accept him as special when he returned to Nazareth during his public ministry. The townspeople felt they knew who he really was, namely "the carpenter, the son of Mary" (Mark 6:3). Jesus later declared that prophets did not receive honor among those who thought they knew them. As with most prophets, those who knew them as they grew from youth to adulthood viewed them as no different from the rest of the people. Because his neighbors thought they knew him so well, they missed an opportunity to get to know and love Jesus, the Son of God become human.

The Son of Man

Among the titles used for Jesus in the New Testament, the title "Son of Man" causes the greatest amount of confusion for many. The problem is that the title is used in so many different ways in the writing of the Gospels. Many commentators believe Jesus used this term in referring to himself. Even if this is true, we must consider the fact that the Gospel writers also used the title in places where Jesus would hardly have used it. Before we begin to read the Gospels, we should try to understand some of the uses of this title in the Gospels. In reference to Jesus, the title could mean any of the following:

A Son of Adam: The title was used at times when someone wished to avoid using the pronoun "I." In a roundabout way, a person avoids acting proud or appearing to boast by referring to oneself as a "son of man." Jesus used this title in reference to himself in his human condition when, for example, he spoke of himself as the "Son of Man" with nowhere to rest his head (Matthew 8:20). In the Book of Ezekiel, the prophet is addressed as "son of man" many times: "Son of man, stand up" (Ezekiel 2:1)!

The Messiah: Jesus is the Messiah who brings the message of salvation to the people. In the story of the sower who went out to sow the seed, Jesus called the sower "the Son of Man," that is, the one who plants the word (Matthew 13:37). The divine power of the Son of Man is shown as Jesus forgives sins, since this power belongs only to God. When he cures a paralytic, he addresses the skeptical scribes and says that he does it so "that you may know that the Son of Man has authority to forgive sins on earth" (Mark 2:10).

The Suffering Servant: The title is used often in reference to Jesus' suffering and death. The Son of Man as the Suffering Servant seems to come from Jesus himself. Just as the Suffering Servant of the Old Testament is called to suffer for the good of all, so Jesus, the suffering Son of Man, suffers and dies for all. In this way, Jesus links the title "Son of Man" with the image of the suffering servant. We read Jesus' words in Mark's Gospel: "He began to teach them that the Son of Man must suffer greatly and be rejected..." (Mark 8:31).

The Eschatological King: Daniel, an Old Testament prophet, spoke of "one like the Son of Man" coming on clouds before the "Ancient One" from whom he receives "dominion, splendor, and kingship" (Daniel 7:13–14). This is an image of Israel that Daniel presented as a type of person. The Gospels portray Jesus as the new Israel and the "Son of Man" sending his angels to "collect out of his kingdom all who cause others to sin and all evildoers" (Matthew 13:41). It is not certain that Jesus intended to claim for himself the role of eschatological king by referring to himself as the Son of Man. It seems more likely that the early Church community, in light of the resurrection, was able to understand Jesus as the eschatological king. The author of the Gospel passed this understanding on to those reading the Gospel.

Understanding the Use of the Title

Although we are able to reduce the title "Son of Man" to several categories, these groupings overlap in such a way as to add to the confusion. Jesus may have addressed himself as the "Son of Man" with one meaning during his lifetime, and the title could have taken on a different meaning in the writing of the Gospels. In order to understand the message behind the title, we should look at its use in the context of the Gospels. The message the writers wished to share, under the influence of the Holy Spirit, is the message we are meant to grasp in our reading of the text.

The Kingdom of God

In the United States, we have a difficult time trying to understand the importance of the idea of a kingdom. As we look to England, for example, we discover the central role played by the monarchs of England in that country's cultural heritage. They currently lack the political control they once had, but they remain important to the people of the country. The people of England and the people of many European countries look back to a history of powerful kings and the great respect shown to them. In the United States, we know the meaning of "kingdom," but we lack the enthusiasm and spirit shown by people more closely aligned with their regal heritage.

The New Testament speaks more often of the kingdom of God than does the Old Testament. For those unfamiliar with the idea of a kingdom that touches our daily lives, the term "kingdom of God" could become meaningless, or at least less important. The fact is that Jesus spoke of the kingdom of God as central to his message, and for that reason we should seek to understand the meaning of the term as it developed throughout the history of the people of God and early Christianity. Just as our emotional response to the word "kingdom" differs from that of the people of England, so our understanding differs a great deal from that of the people of Jesus' time.

The Kingdom in the Old Testament

From Abraham to Moses, the idea of a special type of kingdom for the family of Abraham did not exist. The Israelites saw God as the one true God who guided and protected the Chosen People, but they did not see God as a type of king for the people. When the Chosen People settled in the Promised Land, the idea of a kingdom ruled by God began to emerge. The kingdom of Yahweh (God) was the kingdom of Israel.

The Israelites wanted to be like their neighbors who had kings as their rulers. At first, the prophet Samuel, speaking in God's name, tried to resist this request for a king, fearing that the people would put more trust in an earthly king than in God, the true king of Israel. When God finally did give in to the people's call for a human king, the kingdom still fell under the domain of the one true God. The prophets, in the name of God, anointed the kings, thus showing that the power of the kings came from God. Although these men ruled as kings of Israel, they themselves still had to remain loyal to the one true king of Israel.

Not all the kings of Israel were loyal to their call, and some began to turn to false gods by building pagan altars within their kingdoms. The prophets sent by God wanted the kings to turn back to the true king of Israel or face certain disaster. Some repented, while others rejected their allegiance to God. The great king of all of Israel was David. He did not wield the scepter of the greatest political or economic power in Israel's history, but he did hold a place of high esteem and respect among generations to come. From the line of David was to come the new king who would save the Jewish nation.

As the kings of the northern and southern kingdoms abandoned their call to serve the one true God, their kingdoms crumbled. With the Babylonian captivity, the last of the kingly line disappeared and the people began to look for their salvation in a savior who would spring from the Davidic line. They believed that this savior would be a political ruler who would eventually lead the people to a new, independent kingdom.

Some of the prophets looked to the final days as the time for the establishment of the kingdom of God. The name given to this period is the eschatological kingdom, a term that has its roots in a Greek word meaning "the end time." The prophet Daniel spoke of this eschatological kingdom that would exist at the end of time, not only for the land of Israel, but for all peoples. The final kingdom would recognize that the kingship of God extends to the whole world.

The Kingdom of God in the New Testament

When Jesus used the term "kingdom of God," he was not introducing a new idea. He was using a term familiar to Jews of his day. The kingdom of God is the central message of Jesus' teachings. He came to preach the Good News of the kingdom, and he proclaimed that the kingdom of God was at hand. His miracles became a sign that the kingdom of God had arrived, and his parables illustrated various aspects of that kingdom.

When we speak of the kingdom of God, we must be careful not to perceive it as a worldly kingdom that exists in time and space. Jesus is speaking of a different kind of kingdom, one that is spiritual, not of this world. During his lifetime, Jesus continually corrected those who were looking toward a worldly kingdom and who expected a warrior-king messiah to bring about this worldly kingdom.

In the preaching of Jesus, we perceive a tension between the kingdom that is at hand and the kingdom that does not yet exist. Most commentators believe Jesus was referring to the kingdom that exists now and that will reach its final perfection at the end of time. The kingdom of God that exists now is the presence of Jesus in creation. At the birth of Jesus, this presence broke in upon creation to make the kingdom a greater reality among us. In the death, resurrection, and ascension of Jesus, this kingdom touches everyone through the gifts, especially the gifts of baptism and Eucharist, flowing from these great mysteries. As we share in these gifts, we are sharing in the present reality of the kingdom of God in our midst.

At the end of time, when creation reaches its fulfillment, Jesus will present this glorious kingdom, perfectly fulfilled, to God the Creator. Thus the kingdom of God is both present and future. Although the term "kingdom of God" is often used in the Scriptures, Matthew chose to use the term "kingdom of heaven" for the same idea. The author of Matthew was apparently a Jewish Christian scribe who, raised as a pious Jew, did not freely use the name of God.

The Historical Jesus

The faith reflection of the early Church community that gave us the Gospels offers an insight into Jesus that goes beyond what humans see. We know that the "word became flesh and dwelt among us," but what does that mean? As we look at the humanity of Jesus, we must keep in mind that he was always God, yet totally human. We should never lose sight of either nature.

Jesus' Humanity in New Testament Letters

In many New Testament letters, we discover statements about Jesus that point to his human condition. In the Letter to the Hebrews, the author writes that Jesus was one who was "tested as we are, yet without sin" (4:15, *New Revised Standard Version*). This indicates that Jesus was like us in every way, except for sin. It does not mean that he could not sin; it means he did not sin. The important part of the quotation tells us that Jesus was tempted in every way that we are tempted, which means that Jesus had taken upon himself our human condition to such a degree that he experienced every type of human weakness and temptation that all humans experience.

In another letter of the New Testament, written to the Philippians, the author tells us that Jesus "emptied himself" and became one with us (Philippians 2:7). He took upon himself our human condition. The term used in the Greek points to a weakened, ignorant human condition that we all share in common. Somehow, according to this ancient hymn, Jesus emptied himself of his divine powers and took upon himself our insecure, weakened, ignorant, and struggling human condition. Although he remained God, he accepted a human condition so much like ours that many of his actions were conditioned in the same way as our actions are conditioned. The human image of Jesus found in this ancient hymn does not match the image of Jesus found in many books about his life.

The hymn in Philippians 2:9–11 tells us it was because of Jesus' obedience to death in his human condition that God highly exalted him. In his resurrection and ascension, everyone would bend the knee before Jesus and proclaim him "Lord" in the same manner they would proclaim God "Lord." The early Church recognized Jesus as "Lord" after his resurrection, and they taught this truth through their preaching as though it were constant and recognizable throughout the life of Jesus. The ignorance and lack of understanding of Jesus on the part of the disciples tell us otherwise.

The Gospel Account

The Gospels describe Jesus' human traits that some overlook. In the Luke 2:52, we read that Jesus grew in "wisdom and age and favor" before God and human beings. Some past theories explained this by stating that Jesus knew everything but had to gain experiential knowledge of the world. In other words, although he knew of these things, he had to act them out to gain another type of knowledge about them. In this way, writers tried to preserve the idea of the total God-knowledge of Jesus while at the same time stating he was human. If we accept Jesus as entering into our human condition in the full sense given in the Letter to the Philippians, then we have no need to explain away this text from Luke. Jesus had to learn, although he was totally open to God's word and had a greater understanding of the Scriptures.

The Gospels also portray Jesus as growing tired, sleeping, weeping, eating, acting with anger, telling of his frustration, showing his compassion, looking upon people with love, growing fearful, and suffering pain and abandonment. These are truly human actions. If Jesus lived continually with the heavenly vision of God, he would not have been able to undergo these human responses to life. The pain Jesus felt would have been overcome by the joy that the vision of God brings to those who experience it. If Jesus had this continual vision of God, then he would not have been able to suffer. The beatific vision, as it is called, is so powerful that it overcomes all pain.

Jesus also showed his ignorance on occasion. He openly told his disciples he did not know when the world would end. Only the Father knew. The ability to know all things belongs to God, and since Jesus is God, he should have known this. But Jesus "emptied himself" of this power to know all, and he took upon himself the ignorance of the human family.

One question arising from presenting Jesus in such a human light is: "Did Jesus know he was God?" This question can never be fully answered since none of us has a way of getting into the mind of Jesus. We can say, however, that Jesus, with the human mind that comes with his human condition, could only have known God in a limited way. The understanding that he had about God and the Scriptures would far surpass our knowledge and understanding of God, not because he retained his God-knowledge, but because he was more open to the message and Spirit of God in his life. As the Scriptures tell us, Jesus was tempted in every way we are, but he did not sin. We lack the complete openness to the Spirit of God that is found in Jesus.

Review

✠ What are the many uses of the term "Son of Man" found in the Gospels?

✠ What do we mean by the term "kingdom of God," as it is found in the Scriptures?

✠ What does Hebrews 4:15 tell us about Jesus?

✠ What does Philippians 2:7–11 tell us about Jesus?

✠ What are some human traits of Jesus found in the Gospels?

Reflection

✠ The kingdom of God was central to the preaching of Jesus. How do you understand the idea of the kingdom of God today?

✠ The difficulty in understanding the use of the term "Son of Man" is that it is used in many different ways in the New Testament. Which image of Jesus would you prefer in your relationship with Jesus?

✠ Jesus became fully human for our sake. What does the human image of Jesus as presented in this section mean to you in your daily life?

II. THE ESSENTIALS OF JESUS' LIFE

Jesus is our eternal high priest, yet he became weak to show his astounding love for us. The Book of Hebrews says: "For we do not have a high priest who is unable to sympathize with our weaknesses, but we have one who in every respect has been tested as we are, yet without sin" (Hebrews 4:15, NRSV). Look how much God loved us.

God's Astounding Love

For some people, the thought that Jesus "emptied himself" to become a full member of our human family is difficult to accept, especially when it means that Jesus did not have a full understanding of himself as God. Those who accept the Gospels as biographies of Jesus have the image of a strong, self-assured person who could perform divine deeds whenever he wished. To think otherwise would present us with an image of a weak Jesus, and this, for many, is hard to accept.

From another angle, the image of Jesus who emptied himself to accept our human condition points to a far greater love on the part of God than we can ever imagine. To become human and at the same time retain all the powers of God would at least assure Jesus of some refuge from the difficulties of our human condition. But to become human without retaining all the powers of God leaves one at the mercy of the human condition. It is a far greater sacrifice, and thus a far greater act of love, to accept all the weaknesses of being human. Rather than saying less about Jesus when we place him fully at the center of our human family with all its weaknesses, we are actually saying much more about his love for us.

Developments in Scripture Studies

As often happens with many developments in Scripture studies and theology, scholars have been discussing certain issues long before knowledge of the discussion reaches the majority of the faithful. The study of the weakness of Jesus' humanity is not something that has come forward in the past few decades. It is a study that began before the turn of the twentieth century, with scholars rejecting some theories and accepting others with the passage of time.

In the nineteenth century, many books on the life of Jesus appeared. The basic ideas for the books were that a person could gather enough details from the Gospels to write an accurate biography of Jesus. The authors of these books often made the mistake not only of taking the Gospels as biographies of Jesus, but also of adding their own viewpoint to his life.

Someone interested in moral issues would make Jesus a great moralist, while someone else who was interested in the poor would make Jesus a great advocate of the poor. The particular bias of an author influenced the books to the extent that many different images of Jesus emerged. Many of the writers who treated the Gospels as biographies of Jesus pictured him as God walking this earth in human disguise, as though he was God who simply appeared to be human. That was heresy.

A reaction to this trend came in the form of those who stated that the Gospels were the faith reflection of the early Church community on the life of Jesus. These writers claimed, however, that the life of Jesus found in the Gospels had little or no foundation in real life. The early Church created the events in the life of Jesus to present a true message about the new life brought by Jesus. Such an idea would make Jesus simply a figment a group's imagination and would leave us with little to imitate. The courageous ministry of so many after the resurrection of Christ would make no sense if Jesus had not lived as reported in the Bible. The Church soon rejected this idea.

Our present belief, already stated, holds that the Gospels are indeed the result of the faith reflections of the early Church, but that these reflections are based upon the events and message found in Jesus' life as well as the entire body of Scripture. The writers of the Gospels were deeply influenced by the fact of Jesus' resurrection and the condition of the Church at the time of the writing. When Jesus rose from the dead, he invited his disciples to touch the nail marks in his hands and the wound in his side.

The Life of Jesus

Although we accept the message of Jesus portrayed in the Gospels as the inspired word of God given for our guidance and understanding, we still have the natural curiosity about the person of Jesus in his humanity. With the assistance of deeper research, we are able to draw a composite of the life of the historical Jesus, that is, some of the events and messages that have their foundation in the ministry of Jesus' life.

Jesus Existed

There is no doubt that Jesus existed. An ancient Jewish historian named Josephus, who died around the year AD 100, described the death of Jesus. He identifies Jesus as a wise man, if he could be called a man, who performed a number of good works. He writes that Pilate had him crucified and on the third day Jesus appeared alive to those who received him with affection. Another historian named Tacitus wrote about the year AD 116 that Nero inflicted punishment on Christians who derived their name from Christ, who was put to death by the procurator Pontius Pilate. Most of our information about Jesus comes from the Gospels, and we have certain norms to follow that enable us to give some outline to the life of Jesus.

Jesus Lived in Bethlehem, Nazareth, and Capernaum

It was common in the early Church to state that Jesus was born in Bethlehem, the hometown of his ancestor, David. All four Gospel writers speak of Jesus as living his early life in Nazareth. In Luke's Gospel, Mary and Joseph lived in Nazareth and had to travel to Bethlehem for a census, while Matthew's Gospel places Mary and Joseph as living in Bethlehem at the time of the birth of Jesus. Only later, upon their return from Egypt, does Matthew mention that they settled in Nazareth. Matthew 4:13 tells us that the adult Jesus "left Nazareth and went to live in Capernaum by the sea." Jesus apparently used Capernaum as a base during his ministry.

John the Baptist Baptized Jesus

Jesus began his ministry after the imprisonment of John, and he must have seen in this and in John's later death a foreshadowing of his own fate. John challenged the religious and political leaders of his day. Jesus would not hesitate to challenge the religious leaders. He must have known that this would place his life in danger.

In the early Church period when the disciples were preaching that Jesus was the Messiah, a group of followers of John the Baptist insisted that John was greater than Jesus because John baptized Jesus. This conflict strengthens the belief that John really did baptize Jesus, since the Gospel writers and early preachers would not have invented such a story.

Jesus Preached About the Kingdom of God

The central theme of Jesus' preaching was the new age that was about to begin. Throughout Old Testament times, the Chosen People awaited this new age. In itself, it was not a new proclamation, except for the fact that Jesus announced that it was at hand. The presence of the kingdom of God was the central message of this new age and the central message of Jesus' preaching. Jesus spoke of this kingdom of God through his parables, which not only told the makeup of the kingdom but also identified its gradual growth. A familiar beginning for Jesus' parables was, "The kingdom of God is like...."

Jesus Chose Twelve Apostles

Jesus chose twelve of his disciples to be apostles and live as close companions and followers. These men did not choose to follow Jesus as other people of the day chose to follow some rabbi. Jesus chose them, and they responded to his call. These disciples were chosen to proclaim the kingdom of God. The tragedy of Jesus' life was that one of these close companions would be the one to betray him. All four Gospels speak of the Twelve apostles. They were known as "the Twelve" in the Gospels, an allusion to the twelve tribes of Israel in the Old Testament. When Judas betrayed Jesus, he lost his position among the Twelve, and the apostles had to choose someone to take his place (Acts 1:21–26). Since Christians believe in resurrection, there was no need to replace an apostle if he died. He still held his position as one of the Twelve.

Jesus Challenged Religious Leaders

Jesus challenged the interpretations of the law given by the religious leaders of his day. He came into conflict over the interpretations of the Sabbath law and other interpretations that actually contradicted the law of Moses. Jesus taught with an authority that differed from other rabbis of his day. Where others would quote renowned rabbis of their own era or those of the past,

Jesus spoke on his own authority, without alluding to these other rabbis. The people viewed his teachings and his miracles as a form of preaching with authority. Jesus would give his own interpretation of the law, which amazed the crowd and angered the religious leaders of the day. He especially challenged the leaders for putting their own laws and traditions before the law given by God.

Jesus Was a Miracle Worker

The tradition that Jesus was a miracle worker and an exorcist is too strong to deny. Jesus did perform many healings during his lifetime, and he is portrayed as casting out the evil spirits that caused sicknesses and maladies. Crowds followed Jesus seeking a healing from him. The religious leaders of the day did not deny that Jesus cast out evil spirits, but they tried to undermine his powers by claiming that his powers came from the prince of devils. Jesus pointed out the foolishness of such an accusation. No kingdom divided against itself can hope to survive.

Jesus Preached Throughout Palestine

Jesus traveled extensively throughout a large area of Palestine, preaching his message of the kingdom, healing, and casting out demons. His small band of disciples accompanied him on these journeys. We do not know how many times Jesus visited Jerusalem, although we do know that he was finally condemned to death in that holy city. Like the prophets of old, Jesus journeyed toward the city of Jerusalem with knowledge that the religious leaders hated him so much that they sought to kill him. He was aware of this danger on his last journey to Jerusalem. In fact, his disciples were shocked when he announced that he was going there.

Jesus Endured His Passion

Some of the events of the passion of Jesus showed human signs of weakness that the writers of the Gospels probably would have preferred to omit. After celebrating a last meal with his disciples, Jesus went to the Garden of Gethsemane, where he agonized over his imminent death. Jesus' fear at this time portrayed him in a weak light that seemed to cause embarrassment for the Gospel writers. Although the weakness is there, the writers surrounded the story with signs of strength so as to present Jesus as one who was in total control of the situation. Peter's denial was a special embarrassment for a writer like Matthew, who preferred to present the leader of the apostles in a more kindly light. The flight of Jesus' disciples at the moment of his betrayal also was a sign of weakness that would not have been reported unless it truly happened. At that time, people knew that crucifixion was a common form of torturous death for criminals.

Jesus Was Identified as the King of the Jews

Judas, one of the Twelve, betrayed Jesus to the religious leaders who then held a gathering at night to judge Jesus. To make the gathering legal, a final verdict would wait until the full assembly gathered in the morning. The religious leaders turned Jesus over to the Roman authorities for crucifixion. The title "King of the Jews" was given to Jesus so often during this trial that it was most likely the key accusation against him before Pilate, who was procurator of Judea at the time. This accusation made Jesus liable to death as a leader of a revolution against Rome. We must avoid blaming the Jews as a nation for the death of Jesus. Any sins against Jesus at the time of his persecution and death rest only on the shoulders of those who committed them.

Roman Soldiers Crucified Jesus

Jesus was crucified at the hands of the Romans, and he died without the soldiers resorting to the last painful measure of breaking his knees to hasten death. When people were crucified, they would have to push themselves up on the cross to breathe. The custom of breaking legs was done to make a person smother to death. Jesus was already dead by the time the soldiers would have broken his legs. A secret disciple of Jesus requested permission to bury his body, which had to be done with haste before the beginning of the Sabbath. The Gospels tell us that the women who followed Jesus watched to see where he was buried, since the area had many burial places without markers.

Jesus Was Raised From the Dead

The Gospels tell us that Jesus was raised from the dead on the third day. The resurrection narratives that tell of the reaction of the men and women who followed Jesus are, at best, feeble attempts at describing events that had such a strong impact on their lives. Because of the resurrection of Jesus, his disciples no longer feared for their own lives; instead, they courageously set out to preach the message of Jesus to all nations. No matter how the writers described the events surrounding Jesus' resurrection, they would never be able to share with the reader the intense impact this event had on those who experienced it. First Corinthians 15:6 tells us that more than 500 disciples experienced Jesus' resurrection.

At the end of the Gospel of John, we read: "There are also many other things that Jesus did, but if these were to be described individually, I do not think the whole world would contain the books that would be written" (John 21:25). We have the privilege of learning about Jesus and God's plan of creation and love from the word of God. We really do not need more inspired books than those contained in the Bible. As Pope Benedict XVI says, the New Testament holds the key to understanding the Old Testament, and the whole Bible leads to Christ.

Review

- ✠ What does the understanding of the humanness of Jesus tell us about God's love for us?
- ✠ What were some of the developments in trying to understand the message of the Gospel?
- ✠ What kind of outline could we give for the historical life of Jesus?

Reflection

- ✠ Jesus became a weak human being for us, yet he was always God. What are your thoughts about Jesus being a weak man?
- ✠ The events of Jesus' life tell us a great deal about God's love for us. What event of Jesus' life seems most significant for you to imitate?